USGS
science for a changing world

Prepared in Cooperation with the National Park Service

Significance of Headwater Streams and Perennial Springs in Ecological Monitoring in Shenandoah National Park

By Craig D. Snyder, James R. Webb, John A. Young, and Zane B. Johnson

Open-File Report 2013–1178

U.S. Department of the Interior
U.S. Geological Survey

U.S. Department of the Interior
SALLY JEWELL, Secretary

U.S. Geological Survey
Suzette M. Kimball, Acting Director

U.S. Geological Survey, Reston, Virginia: 2013

For more information on the USGS—the Federal source for science about the Earth,
its natural and living resources, natural hazards, and the environment—visit
http://www.usgs.gov or call 1–888–ASK–USGS

For an overview of USGS information products, including maps, imagery, and publications,
visit *http://www.usgs.gov/pubprod*

To order this and other USGS information products, visit *http://store.usgs.gov*

Suggested citation:
Snyder, C.D., Webb, J.R., Young, J.A., and Johnson, Z.B., 2013, Significance of headwater streams and perennial
springs in ecological monitoring in Shenandoah National Park: U.S. Geological Survey Open-File Report 2013-
1178, 46 p.

Contents

Figures

Tables

Conversion Factors

Multiply	By	To obtain
	Length	
centimeter (cm)	0.3937	inch (in.)
millimeter (mm)	0.03937	inch (in.)
meter (m)	3.281	foot (ft)
kilometer (km)	0.6214	mile (mi)
kilometer (km)	0.5400	mile, nautical (nmi)
meter (m)	1.094	yard (yd)
	Area	
square meter (m^2)	0.0002471	acre
hectare (ha)	2.471	acre
hectare (ha)	0.003861	square mile (mi^2)
square kilometer (km^2)	0.3861	square mile (mi^2)
	Volume	
liter (L)	33.82	ounce, fluid (fl. oz)
liter (L)	2.113	pint (pt)
liter (L)	1.057	quart (qt)
liter (L)	0.2642	gallon (gal)
liter (L)	61.02	cubic inch (in^3)
	Flow rate	
cubic meter per second (m^3/s)	35.31	cubic foot per second (ft^3/s)
	Mass	
gram (g)	0.03527	ounce, avoirdupois (oz)

Temperature in degrees Celsius (°C) may be converted to degrees Fahrenheit (°F) as follows:
°F=(1.8×°C)+32
Temperature in degrees Fahrenheit (°F) may be converted to degrees Celsius (°C) as follows:
°C=(°F-32)/1.8
Vertical coordinate information is referenced to North American Vertical Datum of 1988 (NAVD 88).
Horizontal coordinate information is referenced to the North American Datum of 1983 (NAD 83).
Specific conductance is given in microsiemens per centimeter at 25 degrees Celsius (µS/cm at 25°C).
Concentrations of chemical constituents in water are given in microequivalents per liter (µeq/L).

Significance of Headwater Streams and Perennial Springs in Ecological Monitoring in Shenandoah National Park

By Craig D. Snyder,[1] James R. Webb,[2] John A. Young,[1] and Zane B. Johnson[3]

Abstract

Shenandoah National Park has been monitoring water chemistry and benthic macroinvertebrates in stream ecosystems since 1979. These monitoring efforts were designed to assess the status and trends in stream condition associated with atmospheric deposition (acid rain) and changes in forest health due to gypsy moth infestations. The primary objective of the present research was to determine whether the current long-term macroinvertebrate and water-quality monitoring program in Shenandoah National Park was failing to capture important information on the status and trends in stream condition by not sufficiently representing smaller, headwater streams. The current benthic-macroinvertebrate and water-chemistry sampling designs do not include routine collection of data from streams with contributing watershed areas smaller than 100 hectares, even though these small streams represent the overwhelming proportion of total stream length in the park. In this study, we sampled headwater sites, including headwater stream reaches (contributing watershed area approximately 100 hectares (ha) and perennial springs, in the park for aquatic macroinvertebrates and water chemistry and compared the results with current and historical data collected at long-term ecological monitoring (LTEM) sites on larger streams routinely sampled as part of ongoing monitoring efforts. The larger purpose of the study was to inform ongoing efforts by park managers to evaluate the effectiveness and efficiency of the current aquatic monitoring program in light of other potential stressors (for example, climate change) and limited resources.

Our results revealed several important findings that could influence management decisions regarding long-term monitoring of park streams. First, we found that biological indicators of stream condition at headwater sites and perennial springs generally were more indicative of lower habitat quality and were more spatially variable than those observed at sites on routinely monitored larger streams. We hypothesized that poorer stream condition observed in smaller streams was due to stream drying that occurs more frequently in headwater areas. We also found that biological and water-chemistry measures responded differently to landscape drivers. Variation in most biological endpoints was driven primarily by stream size and was only secondarily associated with bedrock geology. In contrast, water chemistry showed essentially the opposite pattern, with underlying geology explaining much of the variation and stream size being of secondary importance. Therefore, expanding the LTEM program to include headwater areas would yield substantially different biological information, whereas broad inferences regarding spatial patterns in water chemistry would probably not change.

[1] U.S. Geological Survey, Leetown Science Center, Aquatic Ecology Branch, Kearneysville, WV
[2] Department of Environmental Sciences, University of Virginia, Charlottesville, VA
[3] Department of Biology, Lake Erie College, Painesville, OH

Although significant differences in community composition were observed among streams of different sizes, no taxa were unique to headwater sites. All taxa collected at the 45 headwater sites also had been collected at one or more LTEM sites during one or more years. This observation indicates that headwater sites in the park may be structured by biotic nestedness; consequently, focusing management efforts on preserving the species pool at the larger LTEM sites would likely result in the protection of most taxa parkwide. Finally, linkages (correlations) between water chemistry and biological measures of stream condition were significantly stronger when assessed at the LTEM sites than when assessed at the springs or headwater sites, indicating that conditions at downstream sites may be better indicators of water-quality trends.

Introduction

Headwater streams commonly account for more than 75 percent of the total stream channel length in drainage basins (for example, Benda and others, 2004). In addition, headwater streams are critical sites for carbon and nutrient processing, and consequently are important sources of water, nutrients, and species for downstream reaches (Wallace and others, 1997; Peterson and others, 2001). Moreover, headwater sites represent preferred or obligate habitat for some aquatic species (Clarke and others, 2008), and provide dispersal corridors and refugia from natural and anthropogenic disturbances for many others (Covich and others, 2006; Meyer and others, 2007). Despite their importance, however, headwaters are often underrepresented or ignored altogether in biomonitoring and assessment programs, and the implications of failing to incorporate headwater sites into monitoring efforts have not been adequately investigated.

Water resources in Shenandoah National Park (SHEN) include about 90 perennial streams, more than 50 of which support reproducing populations of native brook trout (*Salvelinus fontinalis*) (National Park Service, 1998). In addition, 89 springs have been mapped, and many more are known to exist in the park but have not been mapped (Dekay, 1972). These aquatic habitats together with their associated riparian areas constitute unique and important resources in SHEN, providing irreplaceable habitat for many aquatic and terrestrial species and contributing greatly to the visitor experience of Shenandoah National Park.

Water resources in SHEN are threatened by numerous natural and anthropogenic stressors operating at both local and regional scales. Local stressors include wildfires, ice storms, road salts, water withdrawls, and visitor use. Because of the park's topographic setting at the top of the watershed, however, the primary stressors to aquatic resources are regional in scale and include atmospheric deposition (especially acid-forming compounds of sulfur and nitrogen, as well as mercury), ozone contamination, forest defoliation by invasive pests (for example, gypsy moth and hemlock wooly adelgid), and climate change (National Park Service, 1998).

Long-term stream monitoring in SHEN began in 1979 with the Shenandoah Watershed Study (SWAS) program, a cooperative undertaking of the park and the University of Virginia. The initial objectives of the SWAS program centered on characterizing and understanding changes in water chemistry associated with acidic deposition that was known to be occurring in the eastern United States. Over time, the SWAS program has addressed additional issues that challenge watershed ecosystems in SHEN. The current SWAS watershed data-collection system involves 14 primary study watersheds, including a combination of routine discharge gaging; quarterly and weekly water-quality sampling; and high-frequency episodic, or stormflow, sampling. In addition, a number of extensive stream-quality surveys have been conducted throughout SHEN in support of various research and monitoring objectives (Cosby and others, 2006).

In 1982, the fisheries monitoring program began and was designed primarily to inform park management of the status of the brook trout fishery in the park. The objectives were expanded in 1995 to link the fisheries program with the SWAS program and to provide a biological response indicator of acidic deposition in the park. Consistent with the design of the SWAS program, the fisheries monitoring program was stratified by major bedrock type and ultimately included a set of primary sites (N = 41 sites on 18 streams) sampled annually and another set of secondary sites (N = 87 sites on 71 streams) sampled approximately once every 6 years (Wofford and Demarest, 2011).

In 1984, SHEN was designated a prototype long-term ecological monitoring (LTEM) park. The broad objective of the national LTEM program was to monitor a set of ecological indicators that would characterize the status of and trends in ecosystem condition. Consequently, the selected biological indicators focused on those ecosystem components perceived by managers to be most vulnerable to environmental stressors. At the time of the program's initiation in SHEN, park managers were particularly concerned about the impact of the gypsy moth (*Lymantria dispar*) and acidic deposition on natural resources. The aquatic component of the program focused on benthic macroinvertebrates as a bioindicator of stream condition, and a panel sampling design was implemented that roughly corresponded to that of the fisheries program, with 28 primary sites sampled annually (currently every other year) and another 83 sites sampled on a rotational basis every 3 to 9 years (Wofford and others, 2011).

Taken together, the long-term stream-monitoring effort in SHEN constitutes one of the most holistic (water chemistry, stream habitat, fish and benthic macroinvertebrates) and spatially and temporally comprehensive biomonitoring programs in the country. However, the sampling design of the stream-monitoring program, including water-quality, fish, and macroinvertebrate components, is skewed toward larger stream sites. For example, all 14 primary stream-monitoring sites included in the SWAS program are located on second- and third-order streams whose average contributing basin areas range in size from 230 to 2,370 hectares (ha) (mean = 1,161 ha). Similarly, only 15 (13.5 percent) of the 111 macroinvertebrate sample sites had contributing basin areas smaller than 100 ha (fig. 1A). In addition, although more than 68 percent of the total stream length in the park is first order, only 32 percent of the 111 macroinvertebrate sample sites (n = 36) are located in first-order streams (fig. 1B). Moreover, this estimate is based on stream channels determined from blue lines on U.S. Geological Survey (USGS) 7.5-minute topographic maps, which may underrepresent small streams (Hughes and Omernick, 1983; Leopold, 1994). By using a 15-meter (m) digital elevation map (DEM), we modeled stream channels park-wide using a flow-accumulation algorithm and a stream-origination area of 10 ha. We found that the "blue-line method" underestimates the total stream length in the park by about 30 percent (fig. 1C), indicating that small headwater streams are even more abundant than previously thought. Although it is likely that a substantial proportion of this additional length determined from flow-accumulation models represents intermittent streams, all 40 of the spring sites (see "General Design" in the Procedures section of this report, below) sampled in this study had drainage areas smaller than 10 ha and yet contained water year round, and most had flowing water (that is, they were perennial) throughout the year. Therefore, it is clear that small headwater streams dominate the aquatic landscape in SHEN but are underrepresented in the park's long-term monitoring efforts.

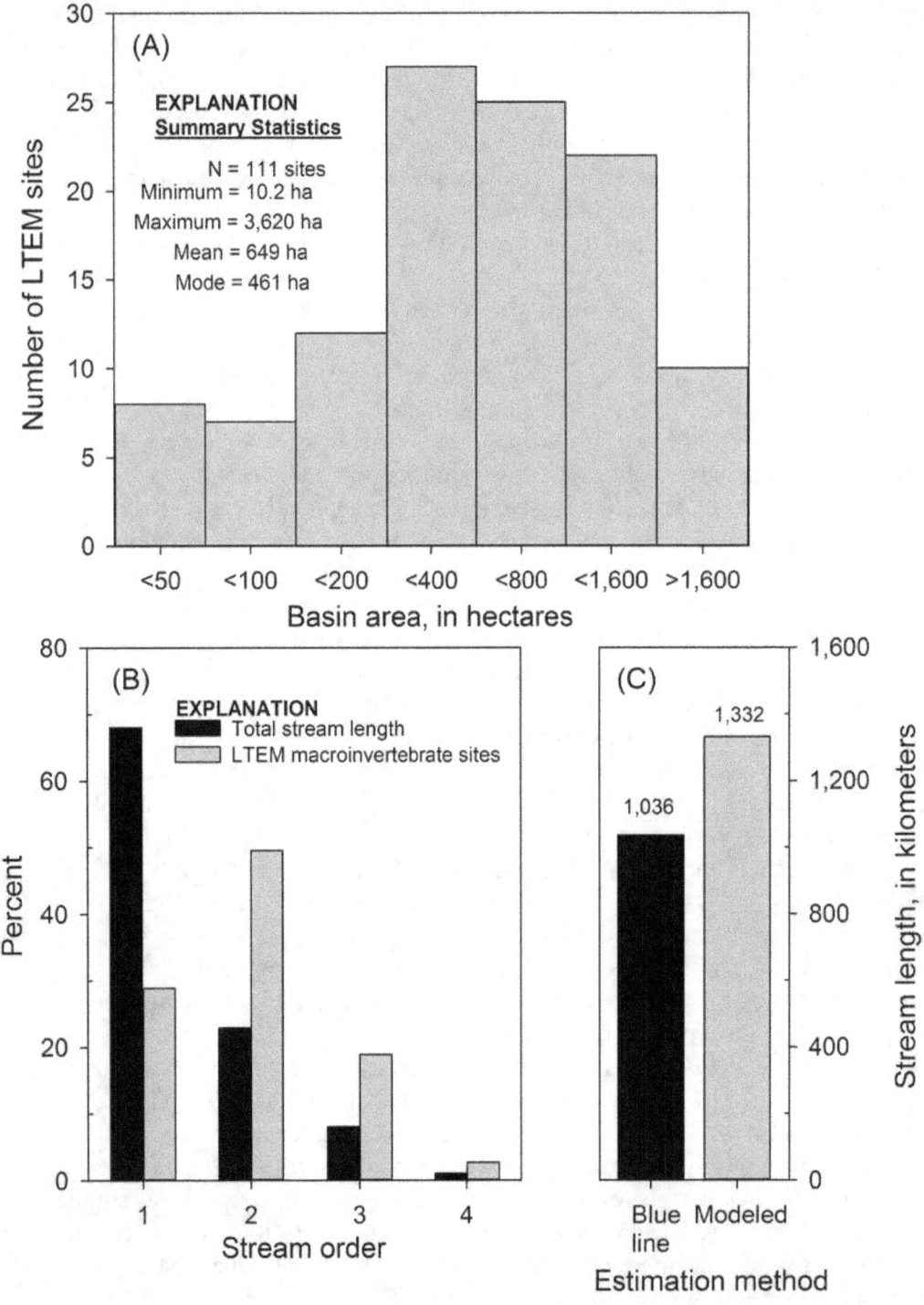

Figure 1. Description of stream sizes in Shenandoah National Park. (A) shows the distribution of long-term ecological monitoring (LTEM) sites among basin area categories (<, less than; >, greater than); (B) compares the total stream length to the number of LTEM sampling sites of each stream order (determined from blue lines on U.S. Geological Survey 7.5-minute topographic maps); and (C) compares the total stream length computed by the "blue line" method to the total computed by flow accumulation modeling.

Failing to adequately represent headwater streams is a pervasive problem in biomonitoring that is not unique to SHEN. Although there are numerous examples of intensive investigation and monitoring of selected small watersheds, few attempts have been made to conduct systematic sampling of headwater streams over large areas (Bishop and others, 2008); consequently, the ability of monitoring programs to provide statistically valid inferences about trends in ecological condition over large areas could be compromised. Underrepresentation of headwater streams in aquatic monitoring programs is due in large part to the numerous logistical challenges associated with routine sampling of these smaller streams at the top of the watershed. For example, as already mentioned, the resolution of available maps is typically insufficient to capture the location and extent of many headwater stream channels. Moreover, even less is typically known about the upstream limits of perennial flow in mapped channels within a basin (Rivenbark and others, 2004). In addition, headwater areas are commonly more remote than downstream areas, thereby increasing the sampling effort (for example, the time required to reach sampling sites) and monitoring costs.

The focus of stream monitoring on downstream areas has also been justified on theoretical grounds. In particular, the linear view of stream systems exemplified by the River Continuum Concept (RCC; Vannote and others, 1980) has provided conceptual support for using downstream sites to evaluate the cumulative condition of watersheds (for example., Cole and others; 2003; Megan and others, 2007). In addition to practical considerations including accessibility and perennial flow, this theoretical concept of downstream sites as integrators of ecological condition was a primary consideration for selecting downstream sites for the long-term monitoring efforts in SHEN. The RCC argues that predictable changes in geomorphology lead to gradual changes in energy sources and, ultimately, aquatic-community structure. Although the RCC has enjoyed substantial empirical support, recent evidence indicates that stream systems often may be more complicated, displaying discontinuities and a "patchy" nature influenced by the geometry of stream networks (Townsend, 1989; Benda, 2004; Grant and others, 2007). These alternative models indicate that the ecological condition of headwater areas may be less strongly correlated with the condition of downstream areas than previously thought.

These recent developments have led SHEN managers and science advisors to question whether the current focus of SHEN long-term monitoring programs should be adjusted or expanded to incorporate more headwater sites. The SHEN Water Resources Scoping Report (WRSR) (Vana-Miller and Weeks, 2004), a review of current and historical research and monitoring of aquatic resources in SHEN, concludes that research on small-stream habitats is necessary in order to fully understand and protect water resources in the park. Specifically, the WRSR called for water-quality sampling at upper stream reaches rather than only at the lower elevation stream reaches routinely sampled through the existing programs. Moreover, additional information presented in the Assessment of Air Quality and Related Values in Shenandoah National Park (Sullivan and others, 2003) indicates that among all surface waters in SHEN, the upper headwater reaches, which represent the largest fraction of total stream length in the park, exhibit the greatest range in chemical and biological properties and the most extreme degree of current impairment and sensitivity to future impairment. The WRSR further recognized that springs and seeps are unique aquatic habitats, supporting biological communities that may be different from downstream habitats, including numerous species endemic to the park, and that these habitats may serve as biological refugia during periods of climate change. Although various sources of information concerning SHEN springs are available (for example, Dekay, 1972; Young and others, 2009; Plummer and others, 2000), more information is needed to inventory and characterize spring habitats. The WRSR recommended further characterization of baseline physical, chemical, and biological conditions in order to provide an informed basis for management and long-term monitoring. This study was designed to address these data gaps.

Objectives

The goal of this study was to characterize the physical, chemical, and biological characteristics of headwater streams and small springs in SHEN. Expanding knowledge of these characteristics will fill a critical information gap regarding the character and importance of headwater areas in the park, and ultimately will inform managers about whether it would be useful to expand the water-resource inventory and monitoring programs in SHEN from the lower stream reaches in the park to include aquatic habitats farther upstream in the headwater portion of individual watersheds. The specific objectives were to--

(1) determine the relations between landscape setting, as defined by topography and drainage area, and the physical, chemical, and biological characteristics of headwater streams and springs in SHEN; and

(2) determine the extent to which the current water-resources monitoring program (which is focused on larger, lower elevation stream sites with larger drainage basins) is representative of the range of aquatic-habitat conditions in the park.

Purpose and Scope

This report compares water quality, benthic-macroinvertebrate community composition and structure, and physical-habitat characteristics between headwater streams and larger stream sites that are routinely sampled as part of existing monitoring programs. We sampled 23 headwater sites that drain approximately 100 hectares, 22 perennial spring sites, and 9 long-term ecological monitoring (LTEM) sites in the park. We also conducted retrospective analyses of long-term data (1987–2006) collected from more than 100 larger stream sites in the park. In addition, three alternative monitoring scenarios are evaluated in the context of the study results.

Procedures

General Design

This study was conducted through a collaborative effort between the USGS and the University of Virginia (UVA). The USGS coordinated and conducted landscape analyses and biological sampling, and the UVA coordinated and conducted water-chemistry sampling. Data analysis and reporting aspects of the study were shared. Biological endpoints focused on aspects of aquatic-macroinvertebrate assemblages, and water-chemistry endpoints focused on characteristics related to nutrients and acidic deposition. Aquatic macroinvertebrates were selected for two reasons. First, measures of the structure and composition of aquatic-macroinvertebrate assemblages have been shown to be strongly tied to the physical and chemical conditions of the site and surrounding watershed (Hynes, 1975). Second, the current water-resources monitoring program in SHEN uses aquatic macroinvertebrates to assess the status and trends in aquatic habitats (Wofford and others, 2011). Water chemistry was selected because of the well-established relations between water chemistry and the distribution and productivity of fish and other aquatic biota.

The project was conducted over a 4-year period (2007-10) that included 2 years of field sampling, 1 year of laboratory analysis, and 1 year of data analysis and reporting. Project objectives were met through the collection and integration of detailed water-chemistry, habitat, and biological data collected from headwater stream reaches at sites draining watersheds approximately 100 ha in size (referred to in this report as "100-ha stream sites" or "headwater stream sites") and from perennial springs, and by comparing characteristics observed in these smaller stream habitats to those measured at larger sites representative of the currently existing program. Historical water-chemistry and benthic-macroinvertebrate data collected over the last 20 years (1987-2006) at SWAS (water chemistry) and LTEM (aquatic macroinvertebrates and stream habitat) sites were also used to provide long-term context.

Landscape Analyses and Site Selection

We conducted landscape analyses to use as the basis for site selection. Analyses involved using geographic information system (GIS) tools to (1) identify all possible headwater stream and spring sampling sites, (2) characterize the landscape setting at all possible sites, and (3) assign identified sites to classes or positions along important landscape gradients. Subsequently, we used a stratified random approach to select sites for sampling. This general approach ensured that sampled sites reflected the range of landscape settings present in the park, and that the studyfindings could be extrapolated to the larger park landscape.

Potential headwater streams were identified by using a combination of existing data and terrain modeling. An existing stream-network map originally digitized by National Park Service (NPS) personnel from the blue lines (indicating streams) on 1:24,000-scale USGS topographic maps (Daniel Hurlbert, Shenandoah National Park, written commun., 2009). Because these maps may not show all headwater streams, however, flow-accumulation modeling was used to construct stream networks throughout the park to identify first-order stream reaches that were not present on the existing stream layer. A 15-m-resolution DEM developed by Young and others (2009) was used for hydrologic modeling. Analysis routines available in the ArcHydro extension of ArcGIS also were used (Maidment, 2002). Because it was expected that many of the first-order streams identified with flow modeling would likely be intermittent, a minimum watershed area was selected on the basis of the distribution of watershed areas of known permanent streams observed through previous studies (Bulger and others, 1995), and only streams identified from the flow modeling that exceeded the minimum threshold were selected. Initially, a threshold of 50 ha was used, but it was found during field-validation surveys in July 2006 (under base-flow conditions) that the water in many of the sites draining 50-ha watersheds dried up completely. Consequently, we selected 100-ha basin areas for potential headwater stream sites. With these methods, 147 potential headwater stream sites with 100-ha (+/- 3 ha) watersheds were initially identified.

The list of potential headwater stream sites was parsed further on the basis of two other landscape factors. First, we included only stream sites for which the entire 100-ha watershed upstream from the site was within the park boundaries; second, we limited the list to sites at which more than 85 percent of the watershed was underlain by a single type of bedrock geology (siliciclastic, granitic, or basaltic). These assessments were accomplished by overlaying the 147 potential site locations on digital maps of park boundaries and bedrock geology (Morgan and others, 2004). We further characterized the landscape setting of potential headwater sites by overlaying site locations on digital maps that depict terrain (Young and others, 2009) so that we could determine elevations at site locations. We classified site elevations into three strata: low, 1,100–1,600 feet (335-488 meters); medium, 1,900–2,500 feet (579-762 meters), and high, >2,900 feet (>884 meters). Ultimately, twenty-three 100-ha headwater sites were selected for aquatic-macroinvertebrate and water-chemistry sampling from the final list stratified by geology and elevation (table 1). No high-elevation sites were in the siliciclastic bedrock geologic type, and only two potential stream sites were in the high-elevation granitic geologic type (table 1).

Table 1. Description of twenty-three 100-hectare stream sites in Shenandoah National Park sampled in 2007.

Geol Strata	Elev Strata	Site No.1	Watershed	Dom. Geol(%)	Elev (m)	Site Coordinates[2]	
						Latitude	Longitude
Siliciclastic	Low	251	Gap Run	100	460	38.32469	-78.63886
		279	Paine Run	100	489	38.20508	-78.77981
		281	Paine Run	100	472	38.19772	-78.77297
	Med	280	Moorman's	100	668	38.20211	-78.74711
		285	Meadow Run	100	619	38.17519	-78.78958
		287	Meadow Run	100	600	38.16306	-78.78942
	High						
Granitic	Low	152	Smith Creek	100	467	38.80800	-78.19311
		179	Thorton River	100	390	38.64314	-78.28106
		192	Dry Run	100	475	38.58433	-78.31714
	Med	181	Dry Run (North fork)	100	654	38.62342	-78.35417
		182	Hazel River	100	705	38.62011	-78.29336
		227	Staunton River	100	632	38.45822	-78.40028
	High	183	Hughes River	100	911	38.61694	-78.33492
		224	Staunton River	100	911	38.46769	-78.41906
Basaltic	Low	148	SF Shenandoah	100	350	38.88772	-78.19931
		161	Dry Run (East fork)	100	468	38.76592	-78.32378
		260	Ivy Creek	100	423	38.27931	-78.63447
	Med	165	Jeremy's Run	100	624	38.74586	-78.31278
		240	South River	100	718	38.37864	-78.50900
		257	Ivy Creek	100	693	38.30100	-78.61878
	High	195	Whiteoak Canyon	84	973	38.57931	-78.37233
		216	Naked Creek	100	919	38.50358	-78.44967
		217	Rapidan River	100	921	38.50214	-78.43731

[1]Site numbers were established for this study and were not used in previous studies.

[2]Site coordinates are reported in decimal degrees and are referenced to the North American Datum of 1983.

Similar methods were used to select perennial spring sites for sampling. Existing data on the location of springs (Dekay, 1972; Plummer and others, 2000; and USGS topographic maps) were used to define potential spring sites for sampling. Where necessary, spring locations were digitized from paper sources (Dekay, 1972; USGS topographic maps), and all spring locations were merged into a single dataset. A total of 83 springs were identified from existing data. A GIS was then used to overlay spring-site locations on geology (Morgan and others, 2004) and terrain (Young and others, 2009) layers to determine underlying geology and elevation for each spring. Only springs with perennial flow were selected. Consequently, in July 2007 (under base-flow conditions), we visited spring sites to verify their presence and to determine their appropriateness for collecting water samples for water-chemistry analysis (water present) and benthic macroinvertebrates (flowing water present). Flow records from the USGS streamgage on the Rapidan River (streamgage 01667500) were used to estimate overall flow patterns in the park. Because flow during the months leading up to July 2007 was unusually low (fig. 2), it is likely that those sites observed to have flowing water in July 2007 are indeed perennial over a large range of weather patterns. However, these sites could be dry during prolonged droughts.

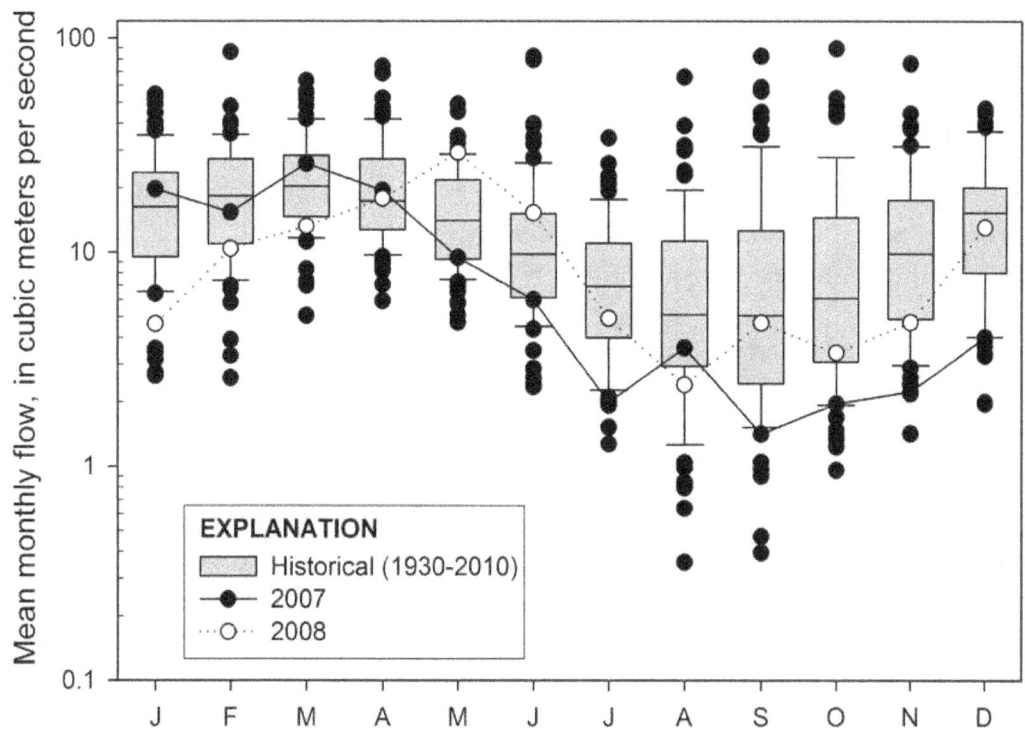

Figure 2. Mean monthly flows for the Rapidan River near Culpepper, Virginia (U.S. Geological Survey streamgage 01667500). Box plots show the distribution of long-term monthly averages (1930-2010), and lines depict montly average flows for the 2007 and 2008 sampling years. For box plots, horizontal black lines within boxes depict medians, upper and lower limits of the box define 50 percent of the values (25th and 75th percentile), whiskers define 90 percent of the values (95th and 5th percentiles), and Individual points represent outliers to the distribution.

Ultimately, 34 perennial-spring sites were selected for sampling and were stratified by geology and elevation (table 2). Because spring sites were concentrated at high elevations, they were not initially classified by elevation. However, sites selected for intensive sampling (benthic macroinvertebrates and water chemistry) spanned the range in elevation observed within each geologic type. Both benthic-macroinvertebrate and water-chemistry samples were collected from 22 sites, and only water-chemistry samples were collected from an additional 12 sites.

Table 2. Description of 34 perennial-spring sites in Shenandoah National Park sampled in 2008.

Geol Strata	Site No.[1]	Spring Name	Source[2]	Elev (m)	Latitude	Longitude	Elements Sampled[4]
Siliciclastic	8	Sawmill Spring (west side)	NPS	479	38.10900	-78.82674	BM, WC
	3023	Blackrock Springs	Topo	594	38.20812	-78.75215	BM, WC
	4004	Blackrock Springs (South)	GPS	615	38.20705	-78.75207	BM,WC
	58	Pinefield Hut	NPS	741	38.29083	-78.64577	BM, WC
	3025	Pond Ridge Spring	Dekay	773	38.15632	-78.76613	BM, WC
	62	Backrock Hut	NPS	796	38.21445	-78.74300	BM,WC
	4003	Cold Springs Hollow	GPS	678	38.18089	-78.78853	WC
	3023B	Blackrock Springs (Lower)	GPS	561	38.26392	-78.75311	WC
Granitic	1898	Old Rag Shelter	NPS	620	38.55445	-78.32956	BM,WC
	1883	Indian Run Shelter	NPS	698	38.82752	-78.16572	BM,WC
	1865	Dickey Ridge Spring	NPS	706	38.83349	-78.17584	BM,WC
	1858	Byrds Nest #3 Spring	NPS	929	38.63659	-78.32017	BM,WC
	3004	Little Hogback East Weir	Dekay	943	38.75589	-78.26933	BM,WC
	50	Bearfence Hut	NPS	943	38.44399	-78.47043	BM,WC
	1876	Hogback Spring #5	NSP	991	38.75898	-78.27234	BM,WC
	47	Rock Spring Hut	NPS	1,018	38.55415	-78.40868	BM,WC
	4002	Old Rag E Ridge Trail	GPS	665	38.55772	-78.30085	WC
	1912	Swift Run Gap #27	NPS	766	38.35444	-78.54893	WC
	3011	Shaver Hollow Shelter	Topo	862	38.61828	-78.35368	WC
	3009	Hazel Mountain Overlook	Dekay	940	38.64429	-78.31509	WC
	3013	Powwow Grounds West Weir	Dekay	1,054	38.58746	-78.38658	WC
	1864	Dean Mountain Gap	Dekay	890	38.38912	-78.51361	WC
Basaltic	3001	Fox Hollow Spring (west weir)	Dekay	547	38.87663	-78.20517	BM,WC
	39	Gravel Springs Hut	NPS	759	38.76416	-78.23342	BM,WC
	196	Ivey Creek Maintenance hut	NPS	791	38.25070	-78.68282	BM, WC
	1895	Matthews Arm Spring	NPS	789	38.75845	-78.30028	BM,WC
	1884	Ivy Creek Shelter Spring	NPS	890	38.26496	-78.65433	BM,WC
	1886	Lewis Mountain Spring #25	NPS	952	38.43317	-78.48232	BM,WC
	3019	Colvin Spring Weir	Dekay	999	38.49220	-78.44899	BM,WC
	3014	Par Springs East Weir	Dekay	1,047	38.58496	-78.38127	BM,WC
	3008	Beahms Gap Spring #2	Dekay	744	38.69724	-78.32248	WC
	53	Hightop Hut	NPS	956	38.33330	-78.55941	WC
	1870	Furnace Spring	Dekay	1,037	38.59736	-78.37951	WC
	4001	Head of Jeremy's Run	NPS	786	38.75864	-78.30027	WC

[1]Site numbers were established for this study and do not correspond to number used by others for same site location.

[2]Source – NPS = map provided by NPS (Dan Hurlbert, SHEN, oral communication, 2009); Dekay = Sites digitized from maps in Dekay (1972); Topo = Spring sites digitized from USGS topographic quadrangles; and GPS = sites located by field crews during reconnaissance for this study.

[3]Site coordinates are reported in decimal degrees and are references to the North American Datum of 1983.

[4]BM, benthic macroinvertebrates; WC, water chemistry.

Although long-term data exist for many LTEM sites, benthic-macroinvertebrate sampling at LTEM sites was not scheduled for 2007 when smaller streams were sampled as part of this study. Therefore, nine LTEM sites were also sampled so that benthic-macroinvertebrate assemblage measures could be compared between LTEM and smaller streams within the same study year, and to ensure that the study year was not unusual. The nine sites were selected from the 111 LTEM sites on the basis of several criteria. First, we wanted to equally represent the three major geologic types underlying watersheds in the park. As with the 100-ha stream sites, only LTEM sites with geologically homogeneous watersheds (that is, > 85 percent of the watershed area is underlain by a single type) were selected. Second, the selection of LTEM sites was limited to those with relatively small drainage areas (that is, < 600 ha) to ensure that inferences regarding "stream type" (surrogate for stream size) effects would be conservative. In other words, if significant effects of stream type were observed when comparing springs and 100-ha stream sites to relatively small LTEM sites, then we could be confident that the chemical and biological condition of small headwater sites was not being represented by the current LTEM sampling design. Third, with the three sites within each geologic type class, an attempt was made to represent variation in elevation. However, meaningful variation in elevation occurred only within the basaltic geology type (that is, within a geology type, LTEM sites tended to be distributed within a fairly uniform elevation). Finally, LTEM sites would ideally represent the park spatially (east to west and north to south).

Water chemistry was also measured at the 14 primary SWAS sites as part of the annual SWAS sampling program. As with the LTEM sites for macroinvertebrates, water-chemistry measurements from the larger watershed SWAS sites would allow for the evaluation of water-chemistry differences between small-watershed headwater sites and larger watershed sites within the same study year. The nine LTEM sites and 14 SWAS sites selected for sampling are described in table 3.

In total, we sampled 80 sites, including twenty-three 100-ha stream sites, 34 spring sites, 9 LTEM stream sites, and 14 SWAS stream sites. We sampled benthic macroinvertebrates at all 100-ha stream sites and LTEM sites, but only 22 of the 34 spring sites. Water chemistry was measured at all 80 sites. Sample sites were defined as 50-m reach lengths for both 100-ha and spring sites. LTEM sites were 100 m in length. We used a 50-m sample reach for the headwater and perennial spring sites because a smaller reach provided at least three riffle-pool sequences whereas the 100-m reach was required to provide a similar number of geomorphic units in the larger stream sites. Sample site locations are depicted in figure 3, and all site locations are attributed in NPSTORET.

Table 3. Description of 9 long-term ecological monitoring (LTEM) and 14 Shenandoah Watershed Assessment (SWAS) sites sampled in Shenandoah National Park in 2007.

Geol Strata	Site No.[1]	Stream Name	LTEM/ SWAS	Dom. Geol(%)	Basin Area (ha)	Elev (m)	Site Coordinates[2]	
							Latitude	Longitude
Siliciclastic	3F105	Lower Lewis Run	LTEM	100	257	460	38.29647	-78.72722
	3L300	Lower Paine Run	LTEM	100	175	562	38.20911	-78.75297
	3L302	Twomile Run	LTEM	100	144	525	38.31117	-78.64953
	DR01	Deep Run	SWAS	99.2	346	412	38.27968	-78.76361
	PAIN	Paine Run	SWAS	100	1271	425	38.19862	-78.79346
	VT36	Meadow Run	SWAS	100	874	468	38.15868	-78.80584
	VT53	Two mile Run	SWAS	100	555	371	38.33392	-78.67114
	WOR1	Whiteoak Run	SWAS	100	512	447	38.25083	-78.74886
Granitic	1L307	Lands Run	LTEM	92.3	172	524	38.82783	-78.18850
	2L308	N. F. Dry Run	LTEM	100	220	507	38.63097	-78.35886
	2L302	Hazel River	LTEM	100	274	682	38.63003	-78.29464
	NFDR	N.F. Dry Run	SWAS	100	235	486	38.63372	-78.35773
	STAN	Staunton River	SWAS	100	1068	309	38.44449	-78.37085
	VT58	Brokenback Run	SWAS	94.4	990	329	38.57052	-78.30444
	VT62	Hazel River	SWAS	100	1126	341	38.61605	-78.26388
Basaltic	1L313	Jeremy's Run	LTEM	100	560	543	38.74886	-78.32381
	2L304	Rose River	LTEM	100	229	863	38.52083	-78.42217
	LIM1	Whiteoak Canyon	LTEM	93.6	234	953	38.57736	-78.37117
	PINE	Piney River	SWAS	69.2	1240	364	38.70178	-78.26776
	VT51	Jeremy's Run	SWAS	70.5	2203	286	38.71555	-78.38144
	VT61	N.F. Thorton	SWAS	71	1898	333	38.69286	-78.27403
	VT66	Rose River	SWAS	87.1	2360	341	38.51541	-78.36624
	VT75	Whiteoak Canyon	SWAS	83.8	1395	349	38.54092	-78.35024

[1]Site numbers are derived from the Shenandoah National Park long-term database.

[2]Site coordinates are reported in decimal degrees and are references to the North American Datum of 1983.

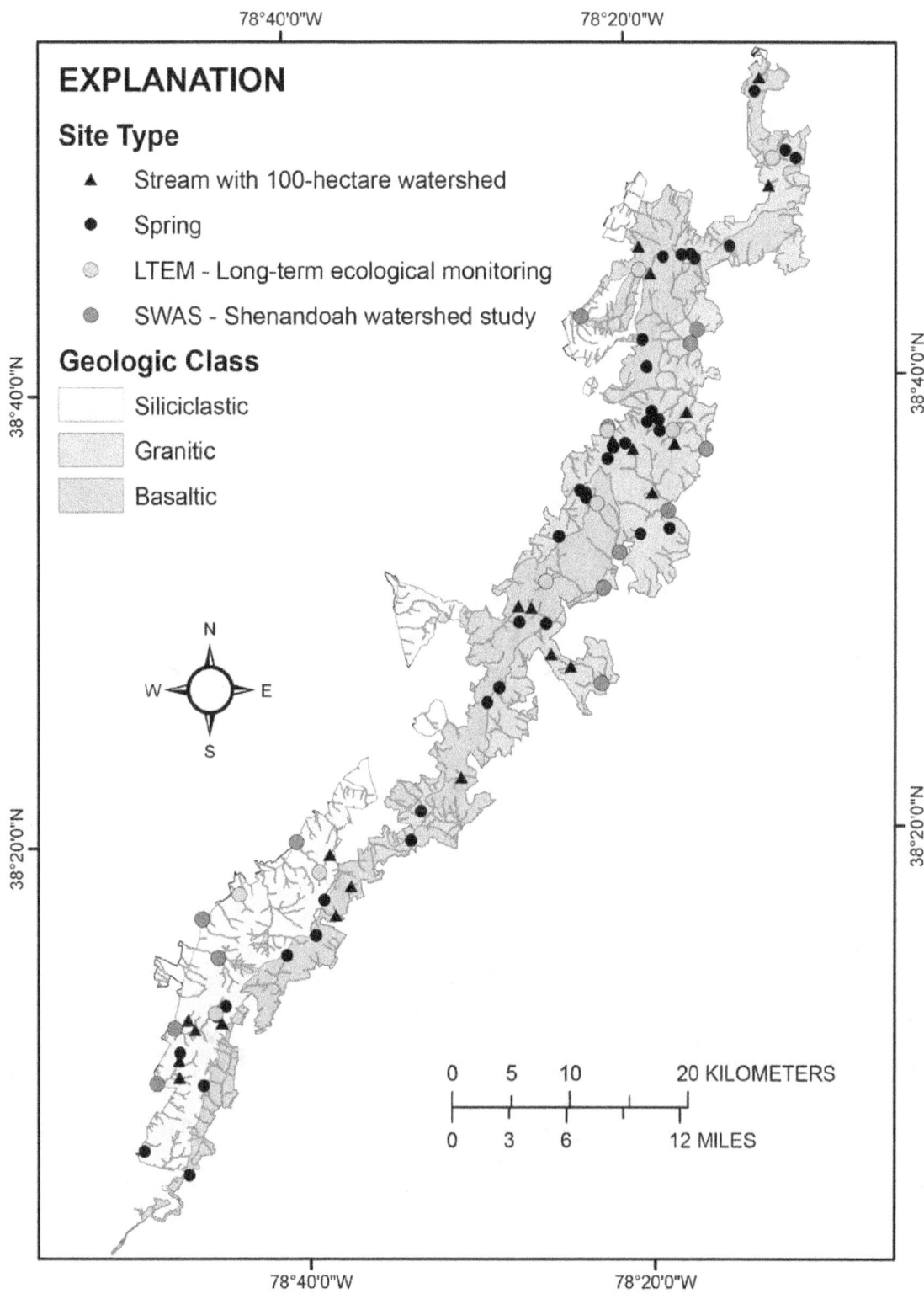

Figure 3. Map of Shenandoah National Park depicting sample site locations.

Sampling Methods

Water samples were collected for chemical analyses at all 71 sites (twenty-three 100-ha stream, 34 perennial spring, and 14 SWAS) during two seasons: early spring (April 7–June 6), when streamflow is typically high, and late summer to early fall (September 29--November 2), when streamflow is usually low (that is, base flow). Spring-season sampling for 100-ha stream and LTEM sites occurred in 2007, whereas spring-season sampling for spring sites occurred in 2008. All late summer to early fall sampling occurred in 2007. For each sample interval, water samples were collected and transported to UVA for laboratory determination of pH, acid-neutralizing capacity (ANC), conductivity, and the concentrations of major cations (Ca^{+2}, Mg^{+2}, K^{+1}, and Na^{+1}) and anions (SO_4^{-2}, NO_3^{-1}, Cl^{-1}). Water samples were collected in prewashed 500-milliliter (mL) collection bottles and maintained on ice until delivery to the SWAS program lab at UVA. Sample preparation and analyses were conducted following methods appropriate for low-ionic-strength water and by methods described in SWAS standard operation procedures for laboratory analysis and quality assurance (Webb and others, 2011).

Benthic macroinvertebrate (BMI) samples were collected in the spring of 2007 at the twenty-three 100-ha stream sites and at the nine LTEM sites, and in the spring of 2008 at the 22 spring sites. The timing of BMI sampling was coincident with spring-season water-chemistry sampling. Sampling protocols were consistent with those used at LTEM sites for more than 20 years (Moeykens and Voshell, 2002; Wofford and others, 2011) except that perennial springs and 100-ha stream sites were sampled with a Surber sampler and LTEM sites were sampled with a Portable Invertebrate Box Sampler (PIBS). Both samplers were equipped with a 350-micrometer collecting net. At each site, three samples were collected at random locations within riffles areas, preserved with 10-percent formalin, and returned to the USGS Science Center in Leetown, West Virginia, for sorting and identification. Macroinvertebrates were picked from samples under 10× magnification, represerved in 70-percent ethanol, and stored for later identification. Macroinvertebrates were identified to the "lowest practical taxonomic level," which is genus level for all insects (except Chironomidae (family level)), family level for all molluscs, and class level for worms. These protocols are consistent with the taxonomic resolution used in the SHEN LTEM program (Moeykens and Voshell, 2002; Wofford and others, 2011). We used Invertebrate Data Analysis System software (IDAS; Cuffney and Brightbill, 2010) to resolve taxonomic ambiguities common to BMI data (Cuffney and others, 2007). In addition, we created a voucher collection that includes at least one representative of each taxon collected. Voucher specimens were processed (preservation and labeling) according to NPS standards.

We conducted habitat assessments in the spring season at the same time as the biological sampling, except for flow measurements, which were made during the late summer base-flow season. For 100-ha and spring sites, we measured channel depth and substrate size at 10 points along the longitudinal profile of the 50-m stream reach (that is, every 5 m). For larger LTEM sites, the 10 transects were located every 10 m along the 100-m study reach and three measurements were made at each transect location to account for the larger drainage area and greater heterogeneity of these reaches. At each sample point, we measured depth to the nearest centimeter with a meter stick and classified the dominant substrate as either silt/detritus (nonmineral, < 6.4 millimeters (mm)), sand (mineral, < 6.4 mm), gravel (mineral, 6.4-50 mm), cobble (mineral, 50-200 mm), boulder (mineral, > 200 mm), or bedrock. Substrate classes were coded numerically (1--6, silt--bedrock) to calculate mean substrate size (Bain and Stevenson, 1999).

We estimated flow in 100-ha and spring sites using the salt-dilution method (Hongve, 1987). This method is designed for assessing discharge in small streams with low flow where more traditional methods are not reliable. Flow at LTEM sites was measured with a Marsh McBirney Flo-Mate 2000 electromagnetic flow meter.

Data Analysis

The main study objectives were met by comparing measures of BMI community composition and structure and water chemistry between the larger, long-term ecological monitoring (SWAS and LTEM) sites and the 100-ha headwater sites and perennial springs. These site classifications represent a gradient in stream size and are hereafter collectively referred to as "stream types."

We summarized BMI community data in two ways. First, we ordinated taxon abundance data (Log10Abundance +1) from all 54 sites where BMIs were collected by using nonmetric multidimensional scaling (McCune and Grace, 2002) to explore broad patterns in community composition among stream types. For these anlayses, we removed rare taxa (that is, taxa that occurred at fewer than 25 percent of the sites (n = 13) prior to ordination. We used the resulting axis scores in further analyses (see below). Second, we computed 15 univariate summary statistics from the BMI taxon abundance matrix for the 54 sites. These summary statistics are widely used to infer stream condition on the basis of community structure and were recommended (Jeb Wofford, Shenandoah National Park, oral communication, 2008) for use in previous analyses. Distributions of all BMI measures were evaluated for normality prior to comparisons and modeling, and transformations were applied where appropriate. The 15 univariate metrics are described in table 4.

For water chemistry, we directly compared pH, ANC, conductivity, and the concentrations of the three anions sulfate (SO_4^{-2}), nitrate (NO_3^{-1}), and chloride (Cl^{-1}). In addition, the concentrations of the four main base cations sodium (Na^{+1}), potassium (K^{+1}), magnesium (Mg^{+2}), and calcium (Ca^{+2}) were added to obtain the sum of base cations (SBC) for comparison among stream types. Prior to analyses, the distribution of each water-chemistry parameter was evaluated for normality. No transformations were required for pH and ANC. The other five parameters were log_{10}-transformed prior to comparisons and modeling.

We used General Linear Modeling (GLM) to assess the influence of landscape setting on BMI community attributes (that is, NMS ordination axis scores and the 15 univariate summary statistics) and water-chemistry parameters. The landscape-setting variables included stream type, geology, and site elevation as main effects. Stream type (perennial spring, 100-ha stream, larger LTEM or SWAS stream site) and geology (siliciclastic, granitic, or basaltic) were class variables and elevation was a continuous variable. We also evaluated all two-way interactions (stream type by geology, stream type by elevation, geology by elevation). As our primary interest in these tests was to explore the relative strength of the relations of numerous response variables to these predictors, we believed it to be unnecessary to use a multiple-test correction such as Bonferroni to adjust significance levels. We also used least-square means computed from GLM models for comparisons among stream types.

An interactive backward selection process was used for model building. We began with the full model (that is, all three main effects and all three two-way interaction terms). We removed nonsignificant predictors one at a time beginning with the interaction terms. For interaction terms that were found to be significant predictors ($p < 0.10$), we plotted the interaction to make sure the relation was not unduly influenced by outliers or points with high leverage. After all interaction terms were evaluated, we used the same procedure to evaluate main effects. This approach allowed us to evaluate the effects of stream type after accounting for the effects of other potentially important landscape drivers, and allowed us to evaluate the importance of stream type relative to these other predictors using partial coefficients of determination (R^2).

The effects of "local" habitat factors (that is, stream depth, base-flow discharge, and substrate-particle size) on biological and water-chemistry response variables were evaluated. Specifically, because it is well established that local habitat is commonly highly correlated with stream size (Frissell and others, 1986), we were interested in evaluating the relative importance of depth, discharge, and substrate size as proximate causes of differences observed among stream types. For this assessment, we substituted mean depth, base-flow discharge, and mean substrate size, one at a time, for stream type and evaluated changes in overall model coefficient of determination (R^2).

Table 4. Description of the 15 macroinvertebrate community metrics evaluated for this study and the expected response of each metric to stress.

[* indicates metric was ArcSin square-root transformed prior to analyses.]

Metric	Definition	Response
Richness	Total number of taxa	Decrease
EPT-r	Number of taxa in orders Ephemeroptera, Plecoptera, Trichoptera	Decrease
EPT%	Percent abundance of individuals of orders Ephemeroptera, Plecoptera, and Trichopera	Decrease
E%*	Percent abundance of individuals in order Ephemeroptera	Decrease
Hydro:T%*	Percent abundance of caddis flies (Trichoptera) in family Hydropsychidae (Trichopera)	Increase
Leuctra:P%*	Percent abundance of stoneflies (Plecoptera) represented by low pH tolerant genus *Leuctra*	Increase
Dom5	Relative abundance (%) of the five most abundant taxa	Increase
SimpsonD	Simpson diversity index (1-D). Measure of richness weighted by evenness	Decrease
PTV	Pollution tolerance value. Weighted sum of total taxa by taxon-specific tolerance values (Klemm and others, 2002)	Increase
Intol%	Percent abundance of macroinvertebrates with tolerance values < 2	Decrease
Scraper%*	Percent abundance of functional feeding group containing "scrapers" (Merritt and Cummins, 1996)	Decrease
Shredders%	Percent abundance of functional feeding group containing "shredders" (Merritt and Cummins, 1996)	Decrease
Hapto%	Haptobenthos. Percent abundance of macroinvertebrates requiring clean, firm, coarse substrates ("crawlers" + "clingers") (Merritt and Cummins, 1996)	Decrease
Chiro%*	Percent abundance of indivuals from family Chironomidae	Increase
SCI	Stream condition index. Multimetric index comprised of eight individual metrics developed for highland streams in Virginia (Burton and Gerritsen, 2003)	Decrease

Assessment of Physical Habitat Characteristics

Two landscape factors, geologic class and elevation, were design variables in the study. That is, we ensured through the stratified site-selection process that there were sites within all three stream types representative of broad patterns in geology and elevation. Moreover, a third landscape factor, drainage area, was explicitly accounted for by stream type itself (that is, drainage area or stream size was the defining basis for distinguishing stream types). However, local habitat characteristics were random variables.

We examined the distributions of base-flow discharge, mean depth, and mean substrate size among sites within stream types to determine whether local habitat characteristics were different among stream types. Not surprisingly given large differences in drainage area, we found large differences in discharge with about an order of magnitude difference in means among stream types (fig. 4). Discharge was highly correlated with stream type (Pearson $r = 0.87$). Mean depth was also significantly higher at LTEM sites than at either 100-ha stream sites or spring sites, and substrate was dominated by cobble at both LTEM and stream sites. In contrast, mean substrate size at spring sites was between sand and gravel (fig. 4). However, both mean substrate and mean depth were also highly correlated with stream type (Pearson $r = 0.64$ and 0.76, respectively), indicating the large influence of drainage area on local habitat.

In contrast to stream type, correlations between local habitat and the other two design factors were weak. Elevation showed a moderate negative correlation with substrate size ($r = -0.49$), but very weak correlations with depth ($r = -0.05$) and discharge ($r = -0.29$). Geology showed weak correlations with depth ($r = -0.15$), substrate size ($r = 0.01$), and discharge ($r = -0.06$).

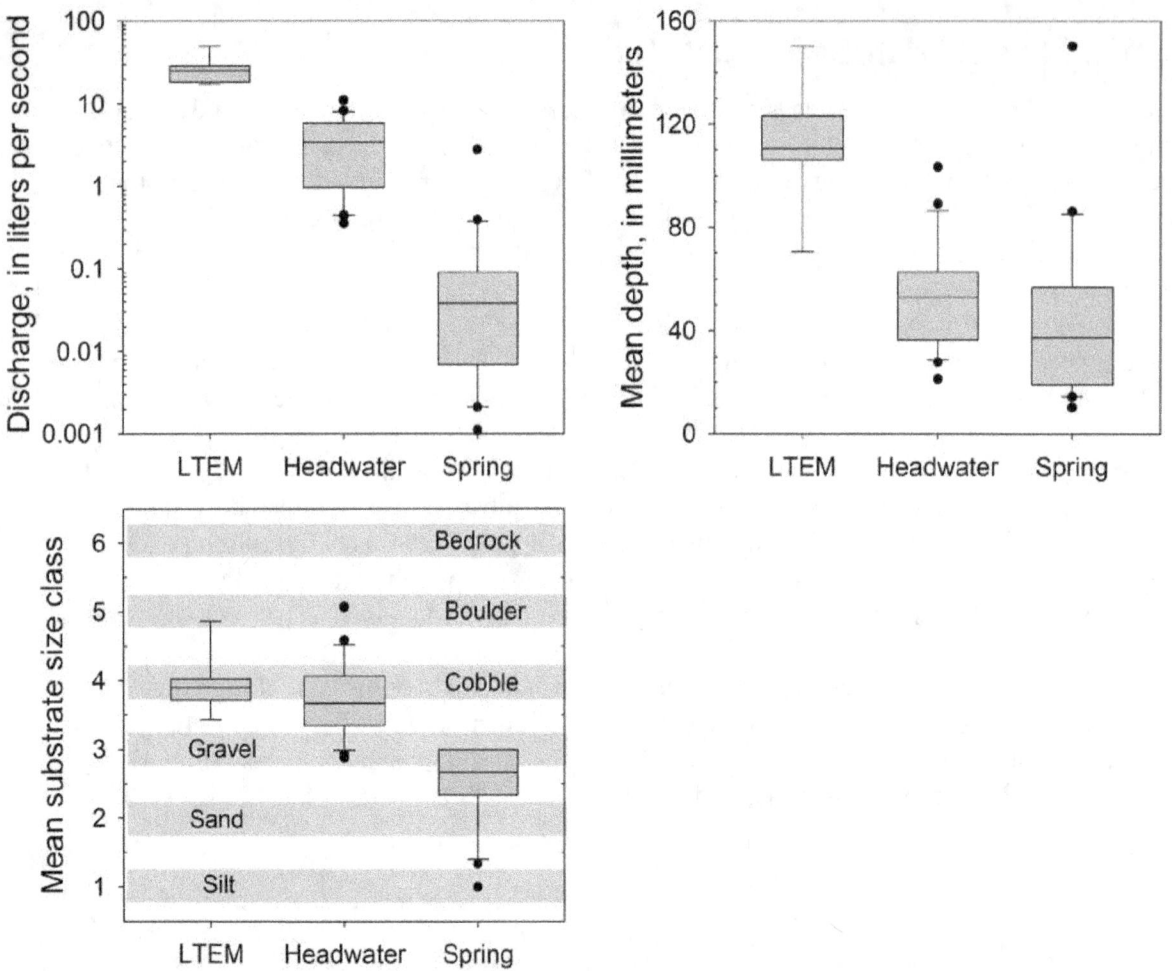

Figure 4. Comparison of local habitat characteristics (discharge, depth and substrate) among sampling site types (LTEM, long-term ecological monitoring; headwater, stream with 100-hectare watershed; spring, perennial spring). For box plots, black lines within boxes depict medians, the upper and lower limits of boxes define 50 percent of the values (25th-75 percentile), whiskers define 90 percent of values, and points represent outliers to distributions.

Assessment of Macroinvertebrate Communities

Multivariate Analysis of Assemblage Composition

We identified 120 unique taxa from 70,994 specimens collected from the 54 sites (nine LTEM, twenty-three 100-ha stream, and 22 spring sites) sampled in 2007 and 2008 (see appendix A). Many taxa collected from springs and 100-ha headwater sites were not collected from the nine LTEM sites in 2007. However, no unique taxa were collected from these smaller sites that had not been collected historically from one or more LTEM sites (that is, over a 20-year period and 111 sites that currently compose the long-term database). Nevertheless, we found substantial differences in taxonomic composition among stream types. Springs supported fewer maylies (Ephemeroptera) and stoneflies (Plecoptera), but more caddis flies (Trichoptera) and non-insect taxa than either 100-ha stream or LTEM sites (fig. 5). In addition, 100-ha stream sites had fewer mayflies and more non-insect taxa than LTEM sites. In general, the proportion of mayflies increased with stream size and the proportion of non-insect taxa decreased with stream size. Trophic composition also differed, with specimens from spring sites composed of fewer collector and scraper taxa and more predators than the 100-ha and larger LTEM sites. The 100-ha and LTEM sites were almost identical in terms of trophic structure (fig. 5).

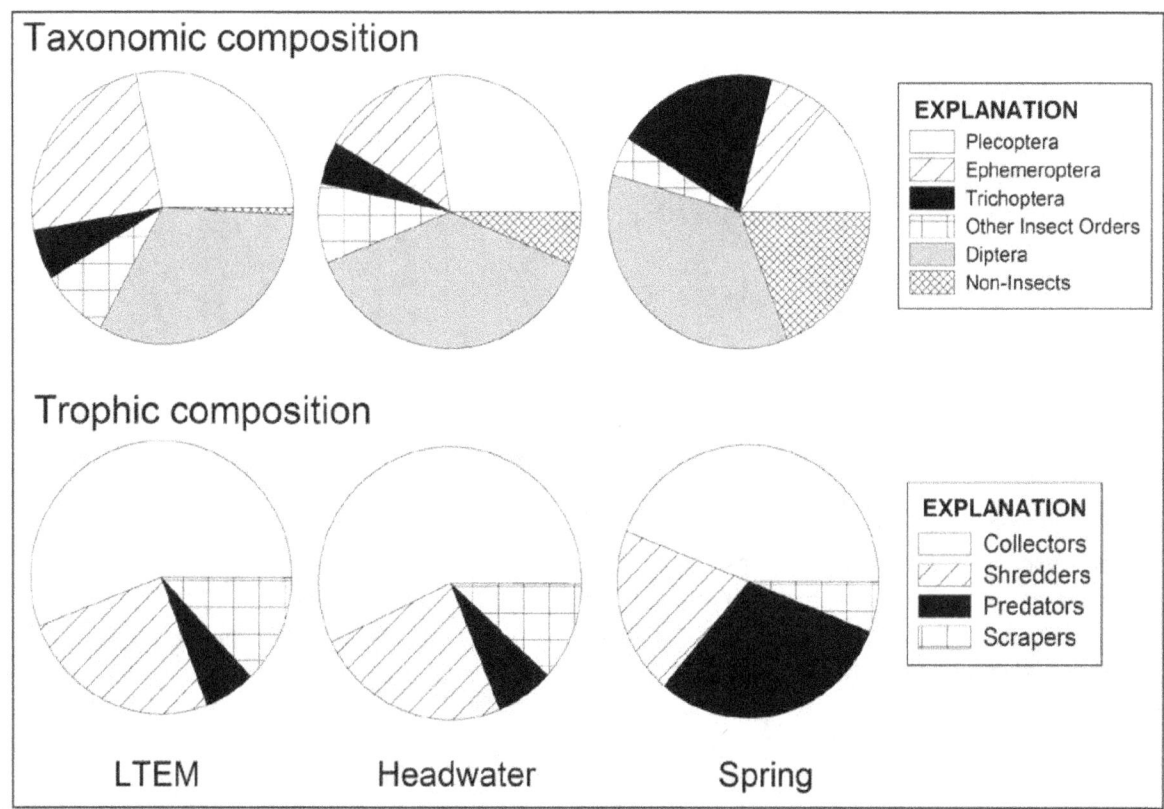

Figure 5. Comparisons of mean taxonomic (top panel) and trophic (bottom panel) composition of benthic macroinvertebrate communities among sampling-site types. Site type: LTEM, long-term ecological monitoring; headwater, stream with 100-hectare watershed; spring, perennial springs.

In addition to taxonomic and trophic composition, we found large differences in patterns of taxa rarity among stream types. The number and proportion of rare taxa decreased with stream size (fig. 6). For example, we found fewer rare taxa at LTEM sites than at 100-ha stream sites, and fewer rare taxa at 100-ha stream sites than at spring sites. We observed this pattern despite the fact that overall taxon richness increased with stream size--that is, total richness increased with stream size (see report section "Univariate Analysis of Community Structure Metrics," below).

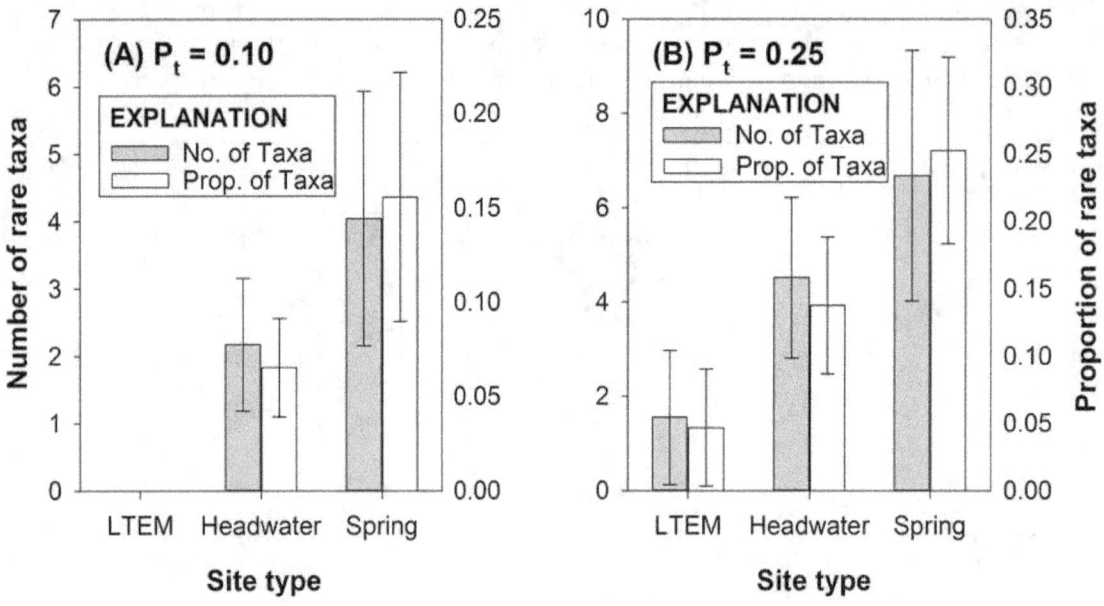

Figure 6. Comparison of the number and proportion of rare taxa (mean+/- 1standard deviation) among sampling-site types: LTEM, long-term ecological monitoring; headwater, stream with 100-hectare watersheds; spring, perennial spring. Rare-taxa thresholds were defined on the basis of occurrence patterns observed at the 111 long-term monitoring sites between 1985 and 2007: (A) P1 = 0.10 (taxa occurred at fewer than 10 percent of the sites); (B) P1 = 0.25 (taxa occurred at fewer than 25 percent of the sites).

We further assessed differences in macroinvertebrate assemblage composition by using ordination. The most parsimonious ordination was a two-factor model (Stress = 17.68, Stability = 0.00001, p = 0.004) that explained 83.1 percent of the total variation in macroinvertebrate community structure. The NMS-2 factor explained far more variation in community structure (65.8 percent) than the NMS-1 factor (17.3 percent). The individual taxa that correlated with each NMS axis are shown in table 5.

The ordination reveals two important patterns. First, in terms of community composition, perennial spring and 100-ha stream sites are distinctly different from communities at larger LTEM sites. All three stream types are distinguished along the NMS-2 (vertical) axis, with scores progressively increasing from spring sites to 100-ha stream sites to LTEM sites (fig. 7). In addition, 100-ha stream sites tend to have lower NMS-1 scores than either LTEM or spring sites (fig. 7). The second important pattern is that variation in site scores is higher for these headwater streams and springs than for the LTEM sites. The range of both NMS-1 and NMS-2 site scores is greatest for spring sites, and 100-ha sites exhibit more variation in NMS-1 scores than LTEM sites, especially along the NMS-1 axis.

Table 5. Taxa showing strong correlations (Pearson correlation r > 0.40) with NMS axis ordination scores.
[Taxa showing positive and negative correlations for each NMS axis are shown separately along with their correlation coefficient in parentheses.]

NMS-1		NMS-2	
Positive	Negative	Positive	Negative
Nigronia (0.524)	*Agnetina* (-0.451)	*Probezzia* (0.737)	*Forcipomyia* (-0.728)
Pycnopsyche (0.438)	*Peltoperla* (-0.522)	*Epeorus* (0.703)	*Molophilus* (-0.701)
Lepidostoma (0.434)		*Haploperla* (0.674)	Gastropoda (-0.668)
Tallaperla (0.427)		*Polycentropus* (0.669)	Oligochaeta (-0.638)
		Acroneuria (0.619)	*Pseudolimnophila* (-0.617)
		Ephemerella (0.602)	*Limonia* (-0.617)
		Oulimnius (0.579)	*Rhyacophila* (-0.563)
		Stenonema (0.563)	*Hexatoma* (-0.555)
		Ectopria (0.543)	*Lepidostoma* (-0.498)
		Pteronarcys (0.529)	Isotomidae (-0.494)
		Psephenus (0.514)	*Pedicia* (-0.494)
		Baetis (0.509)	*Hydrobius* (-0.493)
		Isoperla (0.491)	*Crangonyx* (-0.446)
		Optioservus (0.457)	Sphaeriidae (-0.403)
		Glossosoma (0.432)	*Odontomyia* (-0.402)
		Hydropsyche (0.420)	
		Drunella (0.416)	
		Promoresia (0.410)	
		Antocha (0.408)	
		Leucrocuta (0.406)	

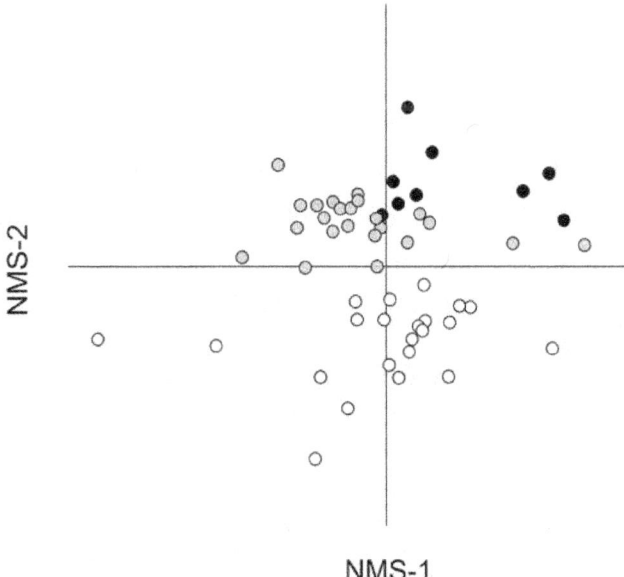

Figure 7. Nonmetric multidimensional scaling (NMS) ordination plot of macroinvertebrate communities from the 54 sites in Shenandoah National Park that were sampled in 2007 and 2008. Black symbols refer to the nine long-term ecological monitoring (LTEM) sites; gray symbols refer to the stream sites with 100-hectare headwater watersheds; and open symbols refer to the 22 perennial spring sites.

We found that landscape factors (that is, the design variables) were highly predictive of NMS-2 scores. Specifically, there was a significant interaction between stream type and geology that, along with their main effects, explained more than 85 percent of the total variation in NMS-2 scores (fig. 8, inset). In general, NMS-2 site scores were substantially lower for spring sites than for either 100-ha stream or LTEM sites, and scores were independent of underlying geology (fig. 8). In contrast, NMS-2 scores for 100-ha headwater streams and LTEM sites depended, to a small extent, on geology, with lower scores for siliciclastic geology (fig. 8). Elevation was not an important predictor of NMS-2 scores.

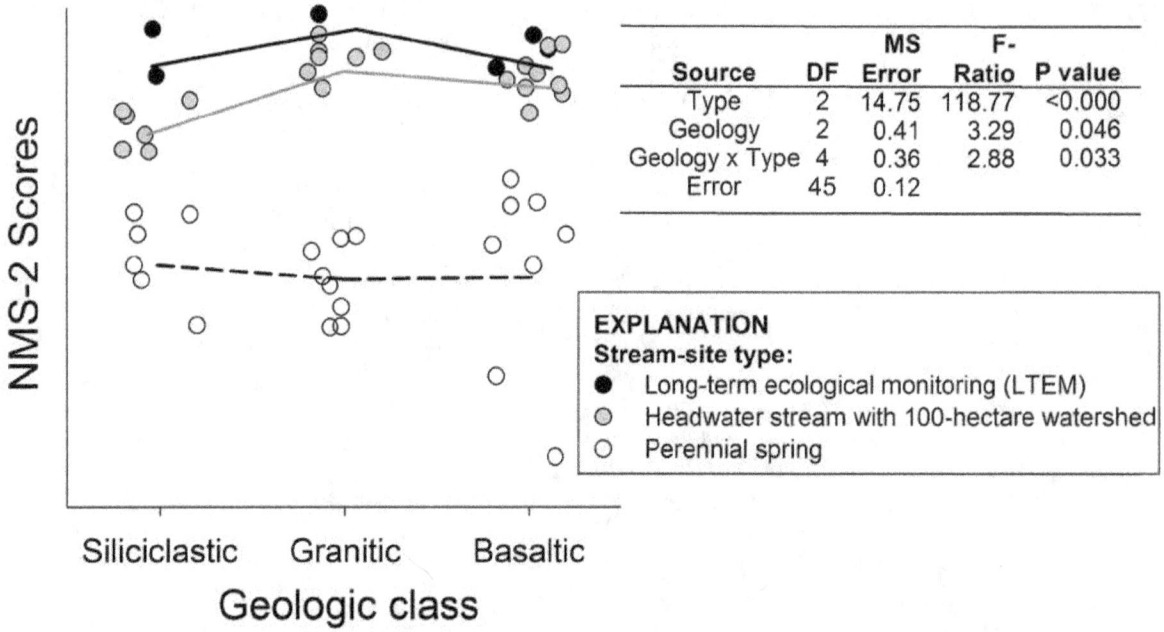

Source	DF	MS Error	F-Ratio	P value
Type	2	14.75	118.77	<0.000
Geology	2	0.41	3.29	0.046
Geology x Type	4	0.36	2.88	0.033
Error	45	0.12		

EXPLANATION
Stream-site type:
- ● Long-term ecological monitoring (LTEM)
- ◉ Headwater stream with 100-hectare watershed
- ○ Perennial spring

Figure 8. Interaction between stream type and underlying bedrock geology on non-metric multidimensional scaling (NMS) axis two ordination scores (see figure 7). Inset table shows analysis of variance results of interactive stepwise general linear modeling: DF =degrees of freedom; MS Error= mean square error. The coefficient of determination (R^2) for the model was 0.855.

Because physical habitat characteristics (that is., depth, flow, and substrate size) were highly correlated with stream type (see discussion of physical habitat above), we substituted mean depth, base-flow discharge, and mean substrate-particle size for stream type in the model (one variable at a time) to determine the most important local factor. We found that substituting discharge for stream type produced an almost identical model, with only a slight reduction in model strength (that is, 5.4 percent less variation in NMS-2 scores explained by discharge than by stream type (fig. 9)). In contrast, substituting depth or substrate size into the model resulted in large reductions in model strength ranging from 31.9 (substrate size) to 50.1 (depth) percent (fig. 9). These results indicate that the effect of stream type on that fraction of assemblage variation associated with NMS-2 is likely associated primarily with flow.

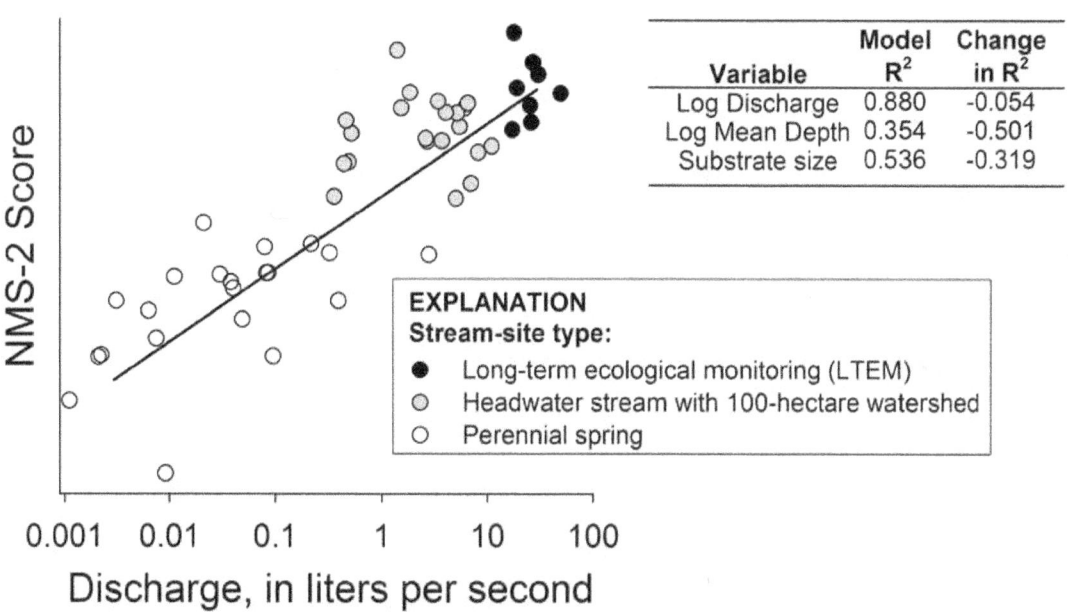

Variable	Model R^2	Change in R^2
Log Discharge	0.880	-0.054
Log Mean Depth	0.354	-0.501
Substrate size	0.536	-0.319

EXPLANATION
Stream-site type:

● Long-term ecological monitoring (LTEM)
○ Headwater stream with 100-hectare watershed
○ Perennial spring

Figure 9. Relation between nonmetric multidimensional scaling (NMS) axis-2 ordination scores (see figure 7) and base-flow discharge. Inset table shows the model coefficient of determination (R^2) for relation between NMS-2 scores and stream-site type; and the changes in model R^2 associated with substituting discharge, mean depth, and mean substrate size for stream-site type in the general linear model.

Landscape predictor variables explained substantially less variation (approximately 34 percent) in NMS-1 scores, (which themselves explained only 17.3 percent of the total variation in macroinvertebrate community structure (fig. 10). Stream type was not an important predictor of NMS-1 scores, but both elevation and geology, as well as the interaction between the two, were significant predictors (fig. 10). NMS-1 scores showed a strong negative relation with elevation, but only for sites draining siliciclastic bedrock geology. NMS-1 scores showed a weaker negative relation with elevation for basaltic sites and were relatively insensitive to elevation in the granitic geologic type (fig. 10).

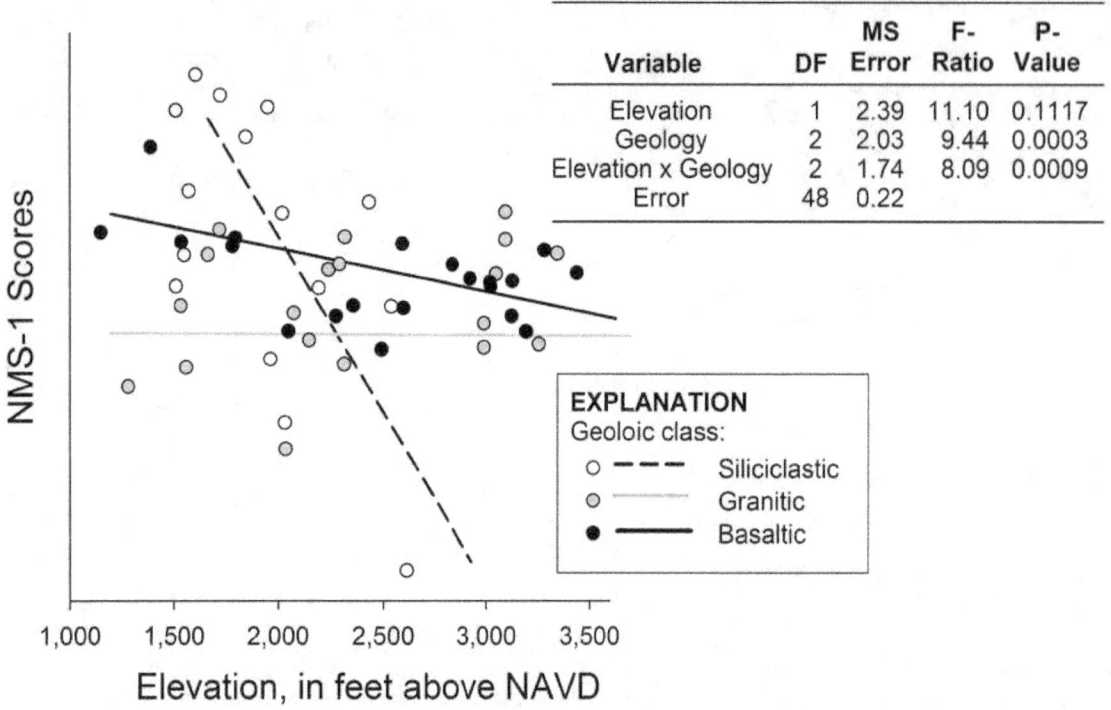

Variable	DF	MS Error	F-Ratio	P-Value
Elevation	1	2.39	11.10	0.1117
Geology	2	2.03	9.44	0.0003
Elevation x Geology	2	1.74	8.09	0.0009
Error	48	0.22		

EXPLANATION
Geoloic class:
○ – – – Siliciclastic
○ ············ Granitic
● ——— Basaltic

Figure 10. Interaction between underlying bedrock geology and site elevation on nonmetric multidimensional scaling (NMS) axis-1scores derived from ordinations (see figure 7). Inset table shows analysis of variance results of interactive stepwise general linear modeling; DF =degrees of freedom; MS Error= mean square error. Coefficient of determination (R^2) for the model was 0.336.

Univariate Analysis of Community-Structure Metrics

We computed benthic-macroinvertebrate community metric values (table 4) for samples collected from all 54 sites (nine LTEM, twenty-three 100-ha stream, and 22 spring sites) in 2007-08. In addition, we computed metric values for samples collected at 24 LTEM sites with long-term data (> 10 years) in order to examine the 2007-08 values with a long-term perspective (fig. 11).

Comparisons of the distributions of metric values among stream types have two important results. First, patterns observed at the nine LTEM sites in 2007 generally were similar to those observed during historical sampling in the park. Mean metric values observed at the nine LTEM sites in 2007 were comparable to long-term means, and the distribution of metric values incorporated a significant fraction of the range of values observed for the larger set of LTEM sites and sample years for most metrics (fig. 11). The second result is that smaller streams commonly exhibited more extreme measures than the larger LTEM sites. Specifically, for 100-ha stream sites, and especially for spring sites, we typically observed values for a single sample year that had never been observed over a 20-year period at the 24 LTEM sites (fig. 11).

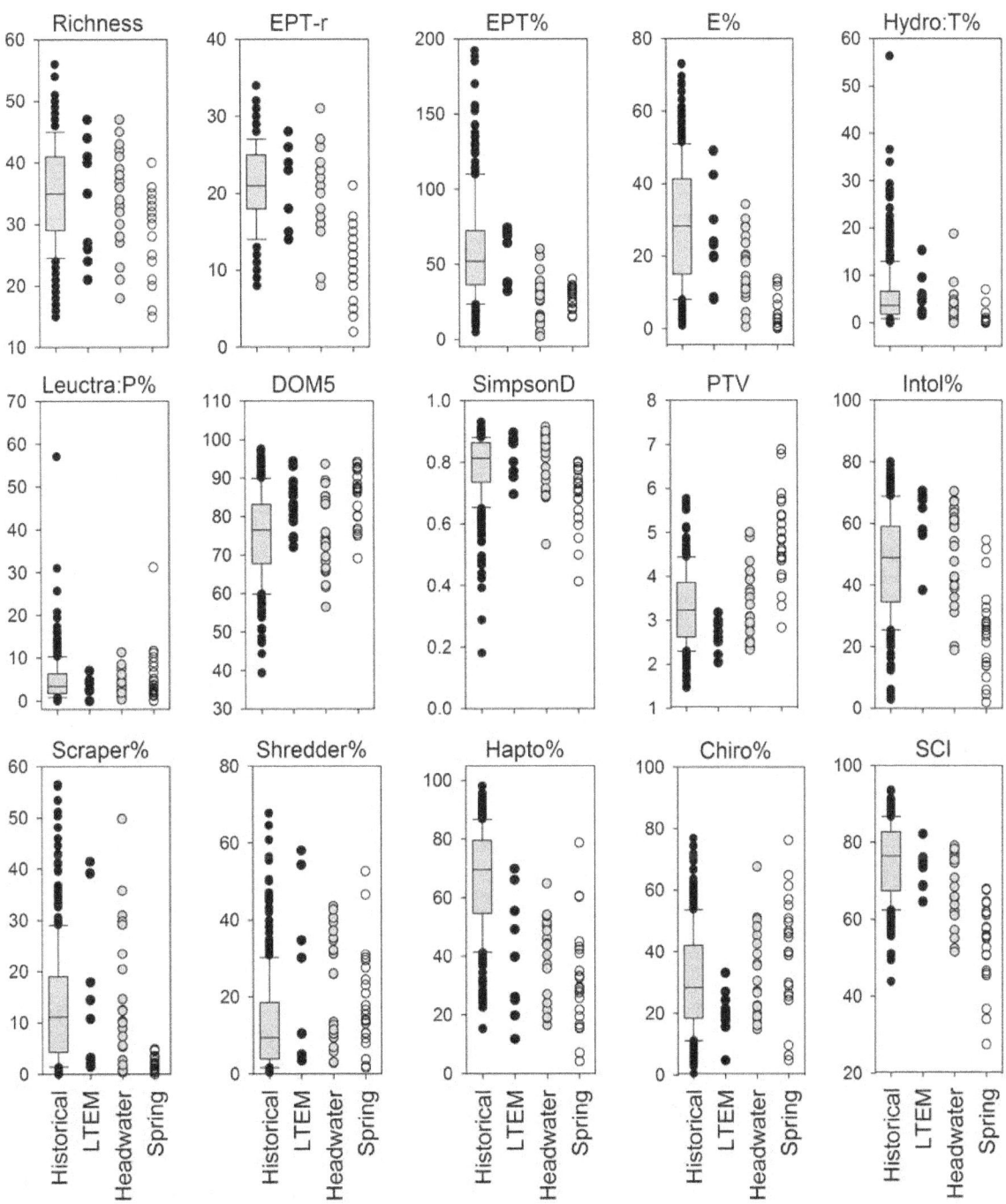

Figure 11. Comparisons of the distributions of benthic macroinvertebrate metric values between long-term data (historical) collected at 24 long-term ecological monitoring sites over the 20-year period from 1987 to 2006 (box plots) and data collected from 9 long-term ecological monitoring (LTEM) sites (black symbols), 23 headwater stream sites with 100-hectare watersheds (gray symbols), and 22 perennial spring sites (open symbols) in 2007 and 2008. For box plots, the horizontal black line depicts the median, the upper and lower limits of the box represent 50 percent of the observations (25th- 75th percentile), whiskers represent 90 percent of the observations (5th- 95th percentile), and remaining values are depicted as points. See table 4 for description of individual metrics.

Stream type was an important predictor of univariate as well as multivariate metric scores, indicating that differences in macroinvertebrate composition among stream types (see report section "Multivariate Assessment of Macroinvertebrate Assemblage Composition," above) translated to differences in univariate metrics and indices commonly used to infer stream conditon. Stream type was a significant predictor of scores for 14 of the 15 metrics evaluated, with only the Leuctra% metric failing to show a significant relation with stream type (table 6). Moreover, stream type was substantially more important than either geology or elevation for all metrics except DOM5 (table 6). In addition, the effect of stream type was more strongly related to base-flow discharge than to either mean depth or mean substrate size, just as we observed for NMS-2 scores. Of the 14 metrics that had significant relations with stream type, the overall model fit (R^2) improved by substituting flow for stream type for 5 metrics. For the remaining 9 metrics, the goodness of fit decreased slightly, although the decrease was less than that observed when either depth or substrate size was substituted for stream type (table 6).

Table 6. Results of interactive stepwise general linear modeling used to assess the effects of study design variables on macroinvertebrate metrics.

[Table reports partial coefficients of determinations (partial R^2) for design variables found to be statistically significant predictors ($p < 0.05$) for each metric, and overall model R^2, and change in model R^2 associated with substituting flow, depth, and substrate size for stream type. NI = "Not interpretable" (main effects not interpretable when interactions are significant; NA = "not applicable (stream type not a signficant predictor)].

Metric	Partial R²						Model R²	Change in Model R²		
	Stream Type	Geol	Elev	Type x Geol	Type x Elev	Ele x Geol		Flow	Depth	Subs trate
Richness	0.211	0.083	0.058				0.352	-0.066	-0.105	-0.070
EPT-r	0.475	0.047	0.040				0.562	-0.042	-0.207	-0.249
EPT%	0.385						0.385	0.020	-0.160	-0.143
E%Hydro:T%	0.559	0.093					0.652	-0.017	-0.254	-0.164
Leuctra:P%	NI	NI		0.141			0.500	-0.049	-0.269	-0.209
Dom5		NI	NI			0.100	0.235	NA	NA	NA
SimpsonD	0.226	0.225					0.451	-0.040	-0.157	-0.11
PTV	0.285	0.117					0.402	-0.099	-0.231	-0.205
Intol%	0.511						0.511	0.041	-0.230	-0.247
Scraper%	0.525						0.525	0.030	-0.198	-0.277
Shredder%	NI	NI		0.109			0.581	-0.006	-0.281	-0.228
Hapto%	NI	NI		0.151			0.363	0.044	-0.096	-0.155
Chiro%	NI	NI	NI	0.133		0.125	0.464	-0.112	-0.164	-0.116
SCI	0.172	0.108					0.280	-0.161	-0.168	-0.165
	0.437	0.033					0.470	0.044	-0.185	-0.253

Geology was also an important predictor of univariate metrics and was included in the "best" model for 12 of the 15 metrics evaluated. However, the observed relations between geology and metric scores were much weaker than those observed for stream type (table 6). Elevation was a significant predictor for only four univariate metrics, and the strength of the associations tended to be weaker than those observed for stream type or geology (table 6).

In order to more fully evaluate differences, we also compared least-square means (that is, mean metric score after accounting for effects of other predictors in the model) among the three stream types for those 12 metrics for which stream type was a significant predictor. We found that means at spring sites differed significantly ($p < 0.05$) from those at LTEM sites for all but 2 metrics (Shredder% and Hapto%), whereas means at 100-ha sites differed from those at LTEM sites for only 2 of the 14 metrics (E% and Hydro:T%) (table 7). In addition, for all but 1 of the 14 metrics, the scores indicated that stream condition was "better" at LTEM sites than at headwater stream and spring sites. Specifically, metric values were higher at LTEM sites for Richness, EPT-r, EPT%, E%, SimpsonsD, Intol%, Scraper%, Shredder%, and SCI (table 7), all metrics that are expected to decline with stress. In contrast, metric values were lower at LTEM sites for DOM5, PTV, and Chiro% (table 7), all metrics that are expected to increase with stress (table 7). The metric Hydro:T% was the only metric that indicated that stream condition may be poorer at LTEM sites than at 100-ha and spring sites on the basis of expected responses to perturbation (table 7).

Table 7. Comparisons of least-square means among the three stream types for 14 macroinvertebrate community metrics found to differ among the three stream types (LTEM, 100-hectare, and springs).
[Table reports means for each stream type along with results of Tukey's Multiple Range test to evaluate the statistical signicance of pairwise differences in means between types.]

Metric	Means			Tukey's Range Test Results (p-values)		
	LTEM	100-hectare	Spring	LTEM=100-hectare	LTEM=Spring	Spring=100-hectare
Richness	34.91	34.79	26.60	0.994	0.022	0.002
EPT-r	21.96	20.45	10.55	0.703	0.00002	0.00001
EPT%	58.90	47.41	27.19	0.166	0.00003	0.0002
E%[1]	25.67	15.95	1.58	0.042	0.00001	0.00001
Hydro:T%[1]	49.75	23.01	5.52	0.027	0.00003	0.005
DOM5	76.33	75.75	85.60	0.980	0.011	0.0003
SimponsD	0.83	0.80	0.67	0.751	0.0009	0.0003
PTV	2.68	3.44	4.94	0.084	0.00001	0.00001
Intol%	61.18	49.54	24.44	0.103	0.00001	0.00001
Scraper%[1]	12.29	11.55	1.76	0.977	0.0005	0.00003
Shredder%[1]	21.66	22.80	18.25	0.981	0.829	0.571
Hapto%	48.71	43.47	34.71	0.624	0.077	0.180
Chiro%	20.37	32.03	40.42	0.121	0.003	0.148
SCI	72.42	68.42	53.41	0.509	0.00002	0.00001

[1]Metric values transformed using ArcSin square-root transformation to normalize data prior to testing. However, back-transformed least square means are shown for comparison.

Assessment of Water Chemistry Patterns

Spatial patterns in seven water-chemistry parameters at 71 sites (fourteen SWAS sites, thirty-four spring sites, and twenty-three 100-ha stream sites) over two seasons (spring and fall). Initially, we tested for the effect of season and found significant differences for four of seven parameters (two-sample T-test, $p < 0.0005$ for all). ANC, SBC, and Cl^- measurements were greater in fall, and SO_4 measurements were greater in spring (fig. 12). That is, seasonal differences in water chemistry did not seem to be influenced by stream type except for SO_4, which showed little difference between seasons at 100-ha and LTEM sites, but which showed higher values in the spring season at spring sites (fig. 12). Therefore, for all remaining analyses, only spring-season data were used for all parameters except SO_4, for which we assessed both seasons separately.

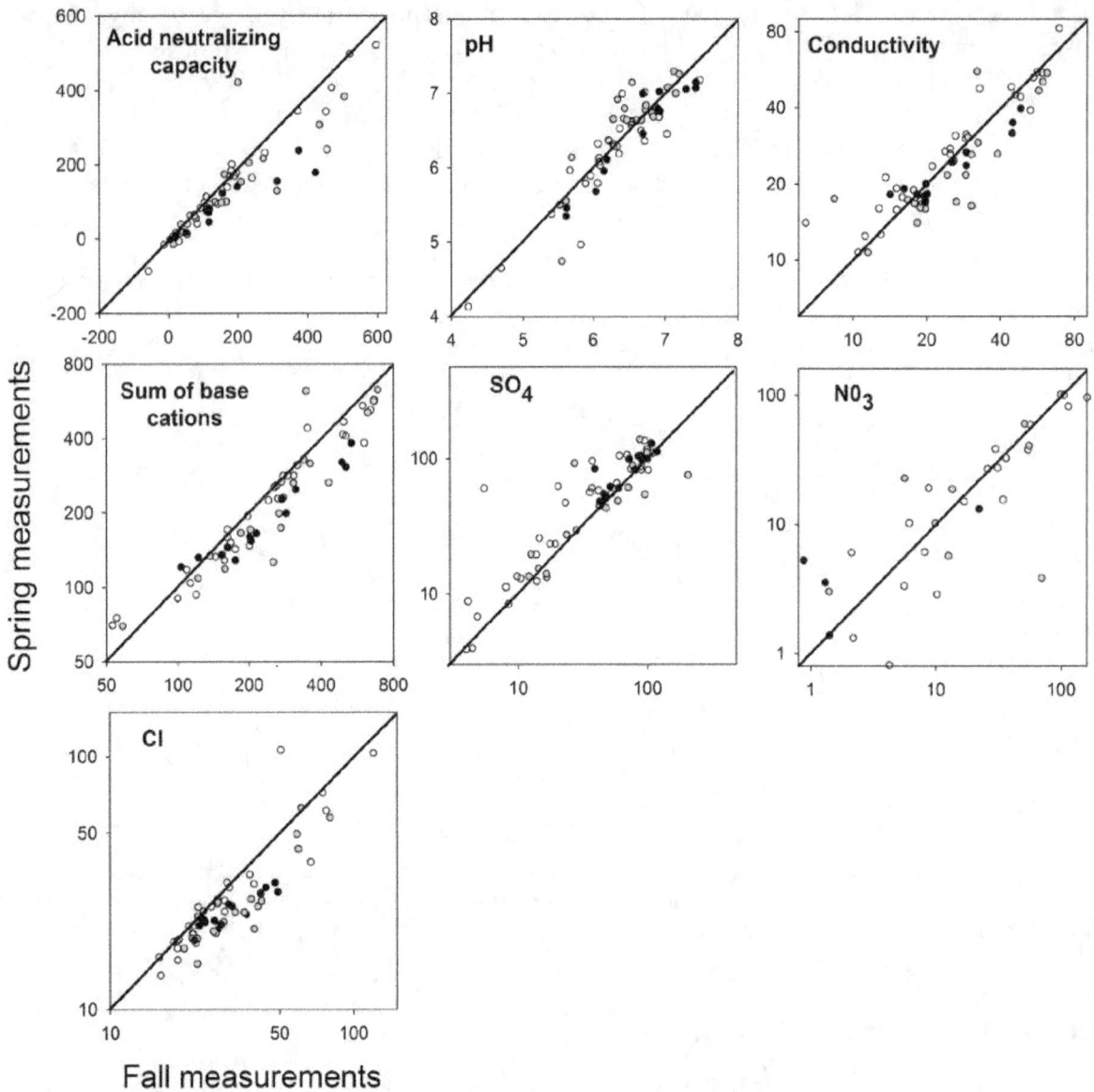

Figure 12. Relationship between fall and spring season water chemistry measurements. Symbol color depicts stream type: black symbol, long-term ecological monitoring (LTEM) site; gray symbol, stream site with 100-hectare watershed; open symbol, perennial spring site. The 45 degree line indicates equal values between seasons; values below the line indicate fall measurements were higher and values above the line indicate spring measurements were higher. Except for pH and conductivity, values are shown in microequivalents per liter; pH is shown in standard units, or the log of the hydrogen-ion concentration; conductivity is shown microsiemens per centimeter at 25 degrees Celsius.

In contrast to macroinvertebrate measures, water-chemistry parameters were much less influenced by stream type. Stream type was an important predictor for only two of the eight parameters. Specifically, stream type explained 6.5 percent of the variation in pH and 10.9 percent of the variation in spring-season SO_4 concentration (table 8).

Table 8. Results of interactive stepwise general linear modeling used to assess the effects of study design variables on water-chemistry parameters.

[Results reported are for spring-season data only, except for SO_4 for which results are reported for both seasons. Table reports partial coefficients of determination (partial R^2) for design variables found to be statistically significant predictors ($p < 0.05$) for each metric, and overall model R^2.

| Metric | Partial R^2 | | | | | | Model R^2 |
	Type	Geol	Elev	Type x Geol	Type x Elev	Ele x Geol	
ANC		0.590					0.590
pH	0.065	0.708					0.773
Conductivity[1]		0.447					0.447
SBC[1]		0.616					0.616
NO_3[1]		0.124	0.361				0.485
Cl[1]		0.176					0.176
SO_4 (Spring)[1]	0.109	0.213					0.323
SO_4 (Fall)[1]		0.169					0.169

[1]Metric values log-transformed to normalize prior to testing.

Underlying geology, however, was an important predictor of all eight parameters and explained substantially more variation, ranging from 12.4 percent for NO_3 to 70.8 percent for pH (table 8), than stream type. Mean pH was significantly lower at spring sites than at 100-ha stream and larger SWAS sites (table 9). Mean spring-season SO_4 concentration was significantly lower at spring sites than at SWAS sites, although differences between 100-ha sites and SWAS sites were not significant (table 9).

Table 9. Comparisons of least-square means among the three stream types for two water- chemistry parameters found to differ among stream types (SWAS, 100-hectare, and springs).

[Table reports means for each stream type along with results of Tukey's Multiple Range test to evaluate the statistical signicance of pairwise differences in means between types.]

| Metric | Means | | | Tukey Range Test Results (p-values) | | |
	SWAS	100-hectare	Spring	SWAS=100-hectare	SWAS=Spring	Spring=100-hectare
pH	6.484	6.420	6.098	0.77130	0.00008	0.00174
SO_4 (Spring)	77.90	53.58	40.72	0.19199	0.00443	0.38618

The strong association between water-chemistry measures and bedrock geology is not unexpected. In fact, a prior understanding of these relations was the primary basis for stratifying site selection when the SWAS program was developed (Cosby and others, 2006; Wofford and others, 2011). Unlike biological measures, mean values of most water-chemistry parameters did not depend on stream type and, for those that did (pH and spring-season sulfate concentration), differences in means among stream types were relatively modest. The general relation between geology and water-chemistry values did not depend on stream type, either (that is, there was no significant interaction between stream type and geology). However, a closer examination of these relations indicates that although mean values did not differ significantly among stream types for most parameters, variation in water-chemistry measurements was substantially greater for the 100-ha stream sites and especially for the spring sites than for the larger SWAS sites (fig. 13).

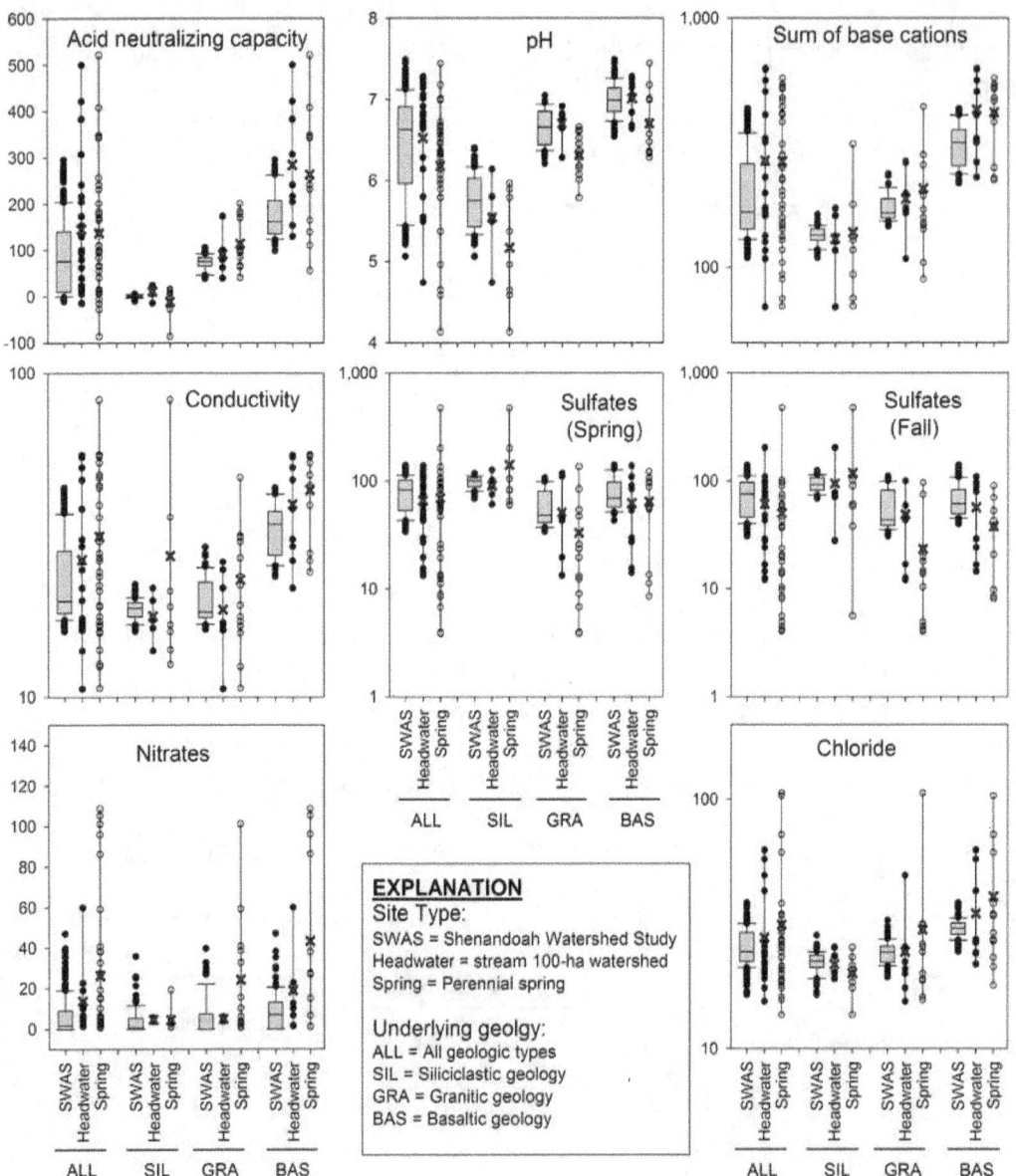

Figure 13. Comparisons of historical water-chemistry measures from larger, long-term water-chemistry monitoring sites (Shenandoah Watershed Study, SWAS) with 100-hectare-watershed stream (Headwater) and perennial spring (Spring) sites. Data for all parameters are for spring season only except for sulfates, where both spring and fall seasons are shown. Comparisons are made at all sites as well as subsets of sites based on geology. Data for SWAS sites were derived from quarterly samples collected from 1993 to 2009 at 14 sites (see table 3), and are shown with box plots. For box plots, the horizontal black line in the box depicts the median, the upper and lower limits of boxes represent 50 percent of observations (25th – 75th percentile), whiskers represent 90 percent of observations (5th – 95th percentile), and remaining values are depicted as points. Headwaters and spring data were derived from sampling in 2007 and 2008 as part of this study (see tables 1 and 2). Individual values are shown as black circles and mean values are shown as "X" symbols. Except for pH and conductivity, values are shown in microequilvalents per liter; pH is shown in standard units, or the log of hydrogen-ion concentration; conductivity is shown in microsiemens per centimeter at 25 degrees Celcius.

Specifically, for most-water chemistry parameters, the distributions of values measured at the thirty-four spring sites and the twenty-three 100-ha stream sites included measurements that were both lower and higher than values in the long-term database for the larger SWAS sites (fig. 13). More extreme values were observed at 100-ha stream and spring sites despite the fact that the dataset for the larger SWAS sites contained significantly more observations (N = 238 compared to 23 for 100-ha stream sites and 22 for spring sites) measured over many more sites and years (14 SWAS sites over a 17-year period). Moreover, this pattern of more extreme values for 100-ha and spring sites was consistent within bedrock geology types as well (fig. 13). Therefore, with the exception of nitrate, for which zero concentration values were relatively common for all three stream types, both the highest and lowest values were observed at the headwater or spring sites. From a water-chemistry perspective, then, headwater stream and spring sites appear to be both more vulnerable and more resistant to atmospheric deposition.

The relation between all seven water-chemistry parameters and geology was essentially the same for all three stream types (fig. 13). That is, the relative differences in means among geologic types were consistent irrespective of stream type. These results indicate that, in contrast to biological measures, water-chemistry values and, consequently, inferences regarding the status and trends in water chemistry would be similar no matter how the sampling effort was distributed among stream types.

Relations Between Water Chemistry and Macroinvertebrate Communities

Given that one of the primary considerations that has driven stream monitoring in SHEN has been concern over changes in streamwater chemistry associated with regional stressors (for example, atmospheric deposition and defoliation due to gypsy moths) and their effects on biological communities, we examined the relative strength of correlations (Spearman's rank correlation, r) between water-chemistry and macroinvertebrate-community summary measures for each of the three stream types (table 10). For these analyses, we only used four of the seven water-chemistry variables because pH was highly correlated with ANC, SBC, and conductivity, and, of these four measures, pH is the most biologically relevant. In general, correlations between water-chemistry and biological measures were stronger at the larger LTEM sites than at either spring or 100-ha stream sites. Specifically, of the 17 biological measures, LTEM sites showed the highest correlation for 12 measures for pH, 10 measures for sulfate, 11 measures for nitrate, and 12 measures for chloride (table 10). Moreover, in nearly all of these cases, correlations were relatively strong ($r > 0.5$). In contrast, 100-ha stream sites showed the strongest correlation for no more than seven biological measures (for sulfate) and spring sites showed the strongest correlation for only four biological measures (for nitrate and chloride); in most of these cases, however, even the strongest correlations were relatively weak ($r < 0.5$).

Table 10. Correlations between water chemistry and biological measures in streams in Shenandoah National Park.

[Table reports Spearman's rank correlation coefficients (r) within each stream type. Values in bold type indicate the stream type (SP = spring site; ST = 100-ha stream site; LT = long-term monitoring or LTEM site) with the strongest correlation for a water-chemistry/biological-metric comparison. Biological metrics include all 15 univariate metrics as well as the two sets of uncorrelated measures of community composition derived from nonmetric multidimensional scaling ordination.]

Bio Metric	pH			Sulfate			Nitrate			Chloride		
	SP	ST	LT	SP	ST	LT	SP	ST	LT	SP	ST	LT
Richness	0.46	0.04	**0.80**	-0.47	-0.47	**-0.63**	0.24	-0.05	**0.90**	0.31	-0.03	**0.83**
EPT-r	0.42	0.03	**0.82**	-0.36	-0.30	**-0.61**	0.18	-0.03	**0.87**	0.22	0.14	**0.85**
EPT%	**0.23**	0.06	-0.20	-0.04	0.08	**0.60**	0.08	-0.16	**0.30**	0.16	0.01	**-0.40**
E%	0.41	0.32	**0.53**	0.00	-0.04	**-0.65**	-0.16	-0.05	**0.60**	0.22	0.16	**0.63**
Hydro:T%	-0.27	0.20	**0.38**	0.12	**-0.37**	-0.02	**-0.31**	-0.21	0.00	**-0.10**	0.01	-0.02
Leuctra:P%	0.00	**-0.25**	-0.10	-0.23	**0.53**	0.15	-0.29	-0.36	**0.90**	0.02	**0.16**	-0.03
Dom5	-0.25	-0.40	**-0.93**	0.06	**0.52**	0.43	0.20	-0.21	**-0.50**	-0.51	0.00	**-0.70**
SimpsonD	0.04	0.24	**0.68**	-0.26	**-0.37**	-0.12	**0.11**	-0.04	0.10	**0.36**	0.02	0.18
PTV	**-0.21**	0.02	0.02	-0.22	0.17	**-0.38**	0.18	0.26	**-0.40**	**-0.20**	0.04	0.15
Intol%	**0.33**	0.02	0.18	-0.10	**-0.24**	0.15	0.06	**-0.17**	0.10	**0.19**	-0.06	0.08
Scraper%	0.34	0.03	**0.78**	0.03	-0.52	**-0.62**	**-0.34**	0.16	-0.10	0.51	-0.22	**0.68**
Shredder%	0.00	-0.40	**-0.55**	0.07	0.08	**0.72**	**0.11**	0.01	0.00	-0.06	-0.17	**-0.78**
Hapto%	0.00	0.07	**-0.58**	0.07	0.37	**0.73**	0.01	**0.17**	0.00	-0.06	0.19	**-0.75**
Chiro%	-0.20	-0.36	**-0.68**	0.29	0.35	**0.77**	-0.30	0.13	**-0.80**	-0.01	0.10	**-0.92**
SCI	0.22	0.21	**0.68**	-0.19	**-0.37**	-0.17	0.19	-0.17	**0.30**	0.24	-0.13	**0.32**
NMS-1	-0.07	0.09	**-0.68**	0.16	0.32	**0.87**	-0.43	-0.14	**-0.50**	-0.07	0.31	**-0.78**
NMS-2	0.08	**0.50**	0.00	0.09	**-0.35**	0.07	-0.26	0.25	**-0.60**	0.06	0.06	**-0.33**

Significance of Headwater Streams and Perennial Springs

The primary objective of this research was to determine whether the current focus of the long-term macroinvertebrate and water-quality monitoring program in SHEN was failing to capture important information on the status of and trends in stream condition by not sufficiently representing smaller, headwater streams. The SWAS water-quality monitoring program does not routinely obtain data for the first-order streams in SHEN. Only 13.5 percent of 111 streams sites that have been sampled as part of the macroinvertebrate LTEM program drain watersheds smaller than 100 ha, and no perennial springs are included. Moreover, only 2 of the 30 sites (6.6 percent) that are routinely sampled (that is, fixed sampling sites) have drainage areas smaller than 100 ha. The program relies largely on measures of aquatic-macroinvertebrate asssemblage structure (a bioindicator of stream condition) and water-chemistry parameters related primarily to acidic deposition to infer the status of and trends in stream condition. In 2007 and 2008, we sampled thirty-four perennial springs (twenty-two perennial springs for macroinvertebrates), twenty-three 100-ha headwater sites, and nine LTEM sites. We also used long-term stream macroinvertebrate and water-chemistry data from a larger number of LTEM and associated SWAS sites (24 for macroinvertebrates and 14 for water chemistry) to address the study objective.

Our findings indicate that biological indicators of stream condition and water-chemistry parameters respond differently to landscape drivers. Variation in most biological endpoints was driven primarily by stream size (that is, stream type) and was only secondarily associated with bedrock geology. In contrast, water chemistry essentially showed the opposite pattern, with underlying geology explaining much of the variation and stream type being of secondary importance. Elevation was not a particularly important driver of either biological or water-chemistry measures. Therefore, a major conclusion of our study is that expanding the LTEM program to include headwater areas would yield substantially different biological information, whereas broad inferences regarding spatial patterns or temporal trends in water chemistry would probably not change.

We found that biological measures of stream condition were higher at larger LTEM sites than at sites in headwater areas indicating stream condition was "better" at LTEM sites. Lower index scores were due mainly to lower taxon richness and higher proportion of relatively tolerant taxa at headwater sites. The data should not be interpreted as reduced stream condition, however, because it is well established that macroinvertebrate diversity increases with stream size from headwaters to mid-reach stream sizes (Clarke and others, 2008, and references therein); consequently, lower condition scores are expected at smaller sites even in the absence anthropogenic stressors. Individual metrics and composite indices are commonly adjusted for watershed size to facilitate comparison among streams of different sizes (Klemm and others, 2003). These adjustments are typically based on regional relations between biological metrics or indices and stream size (usually basin area) in reference condition. However, data from small headwater sites have not typically been available or have been severely underrepresented in establishing these baseline relations. Consequently, direct comparisons of condition measures between headwater areas and sites farther downstream should proceed with caution.

A primary explanation for the positive relation between stream size and macroinvertebrate diversity and abundance is related to the frequency of natural-disturbance events, the relative ability of component taxa to recover from natural disturbances, and how these factors vary across stream size (Vinson and Hawkins, 1998). Stream drying associated with drought is a particularly important disturbance to headwater communities (Clarke and others, 2010). However, because there is a paucity of long-term flow records for headwater streams, little information is available about the frequency of stream drying across a gradient in stream size or basin area. Nevertheless, it is intuitive that stream drying would be more frequent in perennial headwater areas than in downstream reaches, and it is clear that stream drying has a dramatic effect on macroinvertebrate communities that can persist for many years (Feminella, 1996; Boulton, 2003). Moreover, we found stream discharge to correlate more strongly with stream-type differences in benthic-macroinvertebrate community composition and structure than either depth or substrate size, indicating that headwater sites may be more vulnerable to flow-based disturbance.

Recent research indicates that the ability of taxa to recover from stream drying may be reduced for headwater communities as a result of the spatial geometry of stream networks. Specifically, within a drainage network, headwater streams tend to be farther apart from each other than larger order streams (Grant and others, 2007), thereby requiring a longer distance for colonists to disperse in order to repopulate denuded headwater streams. This point is emphasized when aquatic-insect dispersal distances are considered. For example, Griffith and others (1998) found that mean maximal dispersal distances for adult Trichoptera and Plecoptera in four West Virginia headwater streams was less than half the distance among adjacent headwater streams for most species. Hughes (2007) also found limited dispersal of aquatic insects among headwater streams and argued that local extinctions would likely be "final" in many instances. These observations have important implications for biomonitoring. Specifically, macroinvertebrate-community composition and structure measures would be more variable over time because they would be more likely to be in some state of recovery from past natural disturbances. As a result, it may be more difficult to distinguish the effects of natural disturbances from the effects of anthropogenic disturbances in headwater streams.

Another important finding of this study was that although we observed significant differences in community composition among stream types based on taxon abundances, we found no taxa that were unique to headwater sites in SHEN. All taxa collected at the 45 headwater sites also had been collected at one or more LTEM sites during one or more sampling years. This observation indicates that headwater sites in SHEN are structured by biotic nestedness (Cutler, 1994)--that is, the identity of component taxa in the relatively species-poor headwater communities were a subset of the taxa of the more taxonomically diverse LTEM communities. Evidence for biotic-nestedness structure in headwater communities has been reported by others (Malmqvist and Hoffsten, 2000; Heino and others, 2005; Monaghan and others, 2005). This pattern indicates that focusing management efforts on preserving the species pool at larger LTEM sites may result in protection of most taxa parkwide.

As already noted, we did not see significant differences in water-chemistry-parameter means among stream types, and the acid/base chemistry of both springs and 100-ha sites reflected the same general relations with defined bedrock classes as the larger SWAS program sites. However, spatial variability was substantially greater at headwater sites than at larger stream sites for all water-chemistry parameters evaluated. Specifically, parameter values observed at springs and headwater sites tended to include observations that were both lower and higher than values observed in the SWAS site long-term database (resulting in comparable means). This finding was unexpected because headwater sampling was limited to a single year whereas SWAS measurements included more than 20 years of data. However, recent research by others has shown similar patterns. For example, Temnerud and Bishop (2005) found that the range of values for dissolved organic carbon (DOC), pH, and alkalinity observed at 49 headwater sites in two basins was equal to or greater than the range observed in all of northern Sweden in a national survey of hundreds of sites. Similarly, Wolock and others (1997) identified a basin-area threshold of approximately 300 ha in the Neversink River watershed in New York, below which variation in water-chemistry parameters (pH, ANC, DOC, and SBC) was substantially greater than at sites with watershed areas greater than 300 ha.

In general, headwater sites are believed to be more sensitive to atmospheric deposition than larger sites because they have steeper slopes and more rapid runoff (Sullivan and others, 2008), leading to reduced subsurface contact time of rainfall with buffering soils and rock (Wolock and others, 1997). In contrast, recent systematic surveys of headwater areas (Temnerud and Bishop, 2005; this study) indicate that individual headwater sites may be highly sensitive or relatively tolerant of environmental gradients such as acid deposition relative to larger stream sites. These two statements are not necessarily contradictory, however. It may be possible that inaccuracies in the bedrock geology maps could lead to erroneous inferences in water chemistry –geology relations. Specifically, there are strong indications that the coarse spatial grain of bedrock geology maps miss some important features that occur over small spatial scales. For example, it has been observed that basaltic outcrops occur within several of the watersheds classified as underlain by siliciclastic bedrock (Richard Webb, University of Virginia, personal communication, 2007). In this case, the basaltic outcrops could have a substantial influence on water chemistry, leading to water-chemistry values indicative of a relatively tolerant site (for example, high ANC, high pH, low SO_4). The locations and spatial extent of such small-scale features are not typically well known and consequently usually not accounted for in analyses (including our analysis here).

We suspect that these inaccuracies in geology maps would tend to have a larger impact on sites within smaller watersheds because they have stronger aquatic-terrestrial linkages than larger watersheds (Lowe and Likens, 2005). Larger sites are also vulnerable to such inaccuracies, but to a smaller extent. In other words, smaller catchments almost certainly are more sensitive to acid deposition than larger catchments if bedrock geology is compositionally the same. In addition, for some parameters such as chloride concentration, local factors such as proximity to roads (and consequently winter road salts) were likely highly influential on variability. Again, these factors would affect both small and large streams, but would have a larger effect on smaller streams.

An alternative explanation of greater spatial variability in water chemistry at 100-ha streams and especially perennial spring sites relates to the relative contributions of groundwater and surface water to streamflow. Specifically, though groundwater is an important contributor to streams of all sizes in SHEN (Dekay, 1972), the relative contribution of groundwater is greatest in perennial springs and least in larger streams. In fact, many of the perennial springs sampled in this study had virtually no surface drainage area; therefore, all or nearly all of the flow was derived from groundwater. Consequently, water chemistry in these springs may be more likely to be driven by unmeasured factors related to characteristics of the underlying aquifer. Specifically, the boundaries of the underlying aquifer may not correspond to the watershed boundaries (Winter et al. 1998), and the length and complexity of flow paths from groundwater to surface water may be highly variable. Consequently, it is difficult to determine with any certainty the size and underlying geology that influences these systems. For example, unlike for the 100-ha streams and larger SWAS sites, for which we computed the amount of each bedrock geology type in the watershed above the sample site, for perennial springs we noted only the bedrock geology directly beneath the site. It is possible that the underlying aquifer expands widely and a different geology type other than the one directly beneath the spring is more influential. Perhaps even more important, the depth of the underlying aquifer, and consequently the age of groundwater, might also be an important driver of spatial variation in water chemistry (Mulholland, 1993).

These findings have important implications for long-term monitoring for atmospheric-deposition effects on streamwater quality. Expanding the SWAS program to include headwater sites might confound rather than explain parkwide spatial patterns in water quality because of the introduction of "unimportant" variance (such as inaccurate geology) or the incomplete understanding of groundwater/surface-water interactions. Or, because of the greater spatial variation observed, substantially more effort (at higher cost) would be required to effectively characterize natural variability in water chemistry in headwater streams parkwide. Alternatively, a relatively small number of headwater sites might be added to the SWAS program, either to include the areas of the park that are most sensitive to water-chemistry changes associated with acid deposition, or to characterize responses to gradients that vary locally, such as road-salt effects on Cl^{-1} concentrations and associated biological effects.

Finally, the linkages (correlations) between water chemistry and biological measures of stream condition were significantly stronger at larger LTEM sites than at the springs or 100-ha sites. This observation is expected given the disproportionately large role of flow disturbance (especially stream drying) on headwater communities. Specifically, because larger streams are less likely to become dry, the benthic communities associated with them are more strongly tied to water chemistry than those associated with springs or smaller headwater streams. In contrast, because headwater communities respond more frequently to natural disturbances, their relation with water chemistry is obscured. In addition, the finding of fewer sensitive taxa (indicated by lower EPT-r, lower EPT%, lower %Intol, and higher PTV) in headwater areas than in larger streams (also potentially as a result of more frequent natural disturbances in headwater areas) could also mask correlations with water chemistry. Therefore, maintaining the current focus on larger, integrative sites would be likely be most effective with respect to tracking and understanding the biological effects of, or recovery from, anthropogenic disturbance gradients.

Monitoring Implications

In this study, we sampled headwater sites in SHEN for aquatic macroinvertebrates and water chemistry and compared the results with current and historical data collected at larger stream sites routinely sampled as part of the LTEM and SWAS programs. The purpose of the study was to inform ongoing efforts by SHEN management to evaluate the current long-term monitoring program. Specifically, our primary objective was to determine whether the current focus of the long-term monitoring program in SHEN is failing to capture important information on the status of and trends in stream condition by not sufficiently representing smaller, headwater streams. Here we discuss the implications of our results in terms of three possible monitoring scenarios. Although SHEN management may consider alternative objectives, placing our results in this context of these three scenarios should be informative.

Scenario 1: Monitor stream condition as it relates to regional stressors documented to be important at SHEN (specifically, atmospheric deposition and gypsy moths) and their effects on water quality. This is essentially the original monitoring objective cited when the LTEM and SWAS programs were initiated (Wofford and Demerest, 2011; Wofford and others, 2011).

Expanding the current monitoring program to include headwater sites is not likely to yield substantial additional information useful for tracking the effects of regional stressors such as acid deposition. The acid/base chemistry of smaller watersheds reflected the same general relations with defined bedrock classes as that of larger watersheds and, therefore, additional water-chemistry information from smaller watersheds would contribute little to our understanding of spatial patterns or temporal trends in water chemistry. Moreover, variation in water-chemistry measurements was greater at headwater sites than at sites on the larger streams, Therefore, this added variation would be more likely to obscure than to reveal important relations. In addition, relations between water chemistry and biological indicators would be weaker if headwater sites were included in the monitoring program, likely in large part as a result of the influence of natural-disturbance events on headwater communities.

On the other hand, including water-chemistry sampling at headwater sites known to have low ANC or pH or high SO_4 or NO_3 concentration could be valuable in terms of identifying "early-warning" sites. Because this would be a nonrandom selection of sites, however, it may not be appropriate to use these data in the parkwide assessment of status and trends. In the context of this scenario, biological sampling at headwater sites would be valuable only if the effects of natural disturbance could be accounted for, which would necessitate the costly instrumentation and maintenance of a number of headwater sites with streamflow gages.

Scenario 2:   In addition to scenario 1, expand the scope of the current monitoring program to include monitoring for the effects of local stressors such as road and trails, development within the park, ice storms, forest fires, patchy distribution of forest health (for example, hemlock woolly adelgid), and others.

In the context of this scenario, effectively documenting changes in stream condition associated with local stressors would be difficult in the absence of program expansion to headwater areas because much of the development is located in the headwaters. Because this additional monitoring would be extremely costly, however, the use of targeted research rather than monitoring to evaluate these types of local effects could be considered.

Scenario 3: In addition to scenario 1, expand the scope of the current monitoring program to include monitoring for the effects of climate change.

Our evaluation of this scenario is similar to our evaluation of scenario 1. For example, as with acid deposition, small watersheds may be more vulnerable to climate change, and acid-impacted headwater sites may be particularly vulnerable to climate change (Durance and Ormerod, 2007). Therefore, headwater areas may represent sentinel sites for climate change effects. However, as is also the case with monitoring for acid-deposition effects, biological information would be useful only if we could account for effects of natural flow-disturbance patterns on stream communities. Unlike acid deposition, however, climate change is actually predicted to increase the frequency and severity of flow-disturbance events such as droughts and floods. Therefore, in this scenario, flow disturbance is not merely a covariate that needs to be accounted for, but a response of interest. In some regions and ecosystem types, changes in disturbance patterns may be a more ecologically consequential effect of climate change in the nearer term than warming temperatures. Stream drying and flooding events may become more frequent or their timing may become more detrimental to the health of stream communities than gradually increasing temperatures. Therefore, having long-term monitoring sites in highly sensitive headwater areas could be extremely valuable.

Establishing a relatively small number of additional headwater sites for intensive monitoring, including continuous flow and temperature measurements, may be an effective compromise to costly monitoring of headwater sites throughout the park. Locating additional headwater sites within basins that are already more intensively monitored, such as Paine Run, Piney River, and Staunton River, would be a logical expansion of the current LTEM and SWAS programs. This approach provides limited replication and consequently it may not be possible to extrapolate findings to infer park-wide trends. However, with careful site selection, SHEN could be viewed as a sentinel site for effects of climate change in the eastern United States.

We also believe that additional research is needed that is designed to assess the importance of flow variation on bioassessment measures of stream condition. In particular, the temporal pattern of flow-disturbance events (floods and droughts) is likely an important determinant of annual variation in stream-community structure and composition. Therefore, the ability to account for the effects of these natural disturbances may substantially increase bioassessment precision and improve the power to detect change due to anthropogenic stressors (Snyder and others, in press). This is especially important for monitoring programs designed to be early-warning indicators of ecological decline, an explicit goal of the National Park Service Vital Signs Monitoring Program (Fancy and others, 2009).

Acknowledgments

The authors thank the following people for their assistance in collecting and processing samples: Mary Mandt Rockey, David Weller, and Marcus Springmann of the U.S. Geological Survey; and, Spencer Ingram, Shane Spitzer, Ben Sutphen, Zach Lucy and Suzanne Maben of the University of Virginia. We are also grateful to John Karish, James Atkinson, Jeb Wofford, Alan Williams, and James Schaberl of the Shenandoah National Park Natural Resource Management staff for assisting with project development and providing logistical support. Thanks also to Nathaniel Hitt of the U.S. Geological Survey and Amy Villamagna of Virginia Tech University for reviewing the manuscript. This study was conducted as part of the U.S. Geological Survey's Natural Resource Preservation Program.

References Cited

Bain, M.B., and Stevenson, N.J., eds., 1999, Aquatic habitat assessment: Common methods: Bethesda, Maryland, American Fisheries Society, 137 pp.

Benda, L., Poff, N.L., Miller, D., Dunne, T., Reeves, G., Pess, G., and Pollock, M., 2004, The network dynamics hypothesis: How channel networks structure riverine habitats: BioScience, v. 54, p. 413–427.

Bishop, K., Buffam, I., Erlandsson, M., Folster, J., Laudon, H., Seibert, J., and Temnerud, J., 2008, Aqua Incognita: The unknown headwaters: Hydrologic Processes, v. 22, p. 1239–1242.

Boulton, A.J., 2003, Parallels and contrasts in the effects of drought on stream macroinvertebrate assemblages: Freshwater Biology, v. 48, p. 1173–1185.

Bulger, A.J., Dolloff, C.A., Cosby, B.J., Eshleman, K.N., Webb, J.R., and Galloway, J.N., 1995, The "Shenandoah National Park: Fish in Sensitive Habitats (SNP: FISH) Project. An integrated assessment of fish community responses to stream acidification: Water, Air and Soil Pollution, v. 85, p. 309-314.

Burton, J., and Gerritsen, J., 2003, A stream condition index for Virginia non-Coastal streams: Report to the U.S. Environmental Protection Agency: Owings Mills, Md., Tetra Tech, Inc. 76 pp plus appendices.

Clarke, A., MacNally, R., Bond, N., and Lake, P.S., 2008, Macroinvertebrate diversity in headwater streams—A review: Freshwater Biology, v. 53, p. 1707–1721.

Clarke, A., Mac Nally, R., Bond, N., and Lake, P.S., 2010, Flow permanence affects aquatic macroinvertebrate diversity and community structure in three headwater streams in a forested catchment: Canadian Journal of Fisheries and Aquatic Sciences, v. 67, p. 1649–1657.

Cole, M.B., Russell, K.R., and Mabee, T.J., 2003. Relation of headwater macroinvertebrate communites to instream and adjacent forests of the Oregon Coast Range mountains: Canadian Journal of Fisheries and Aquatic Sciences, v. 33, p. 1433–1443.

Cosby, B.J., Webb, J.R., Galloway, J.N., and Deviney, F.A., 2006, Acidic deposition impacts on natural resources in Shenandoah National Park: Philadelphia, Pa., U.S. Department of the Interior, National Park Service, Technical Report NPS/NER/NRTR-2006/066. (Also available at http://www.nps.gov/nero/science/FINAL/SHEN_acid_dep/SHEN_acid_dep.htm.)

Covich, A.P., Crowl, T.A., and Heartsill-Scalley,T., 2006, Effects of drought and hurricane disturbance on headwater distributions of palaemonid river shrimp (*Macrobrachium spp.*) in the Luquillo Mountains, Puerto Rico: Journal of the North American Benthological Society, v. 25, p. 99–107.

Cuffney, T.F., Bilger, M.D., and Haigler, A.M., 2007, Ambiguous taxa: Effects on the charaterization and interpretation of invertebrate assemblages: Journal of the North American Benthological Society, v. 26, p. 286–307.

Cuffney, T.F., and Brightbill, R.A., 2010, User's manual for the National Water-Quality Assessment Program Invertebrate Data Analysis System (IDAS) software, version 5: U.S. Geological Survey Techniques and Methods 7–C4, 126 p. (Also available at http://pubs.usgs.gov/tm/7C4/.)

Cutler, A.H., 1994, Nested biotas and biological conservation: Metrics, mechanisms, and meaning of nestedness: Landscape Urban Planning, v. 28, p. 73–82.

DeKay, R.H., 1972,Development of ground-water supplies in Shenandoah National Park, Virginia: Charlottesville, Va., Virginia Division of Mineral Resources, Mineral Resources Report 10, 158 pp.

Durance, I., and Omerod, S.J., 2007. Climate change effects on upland stream macroinvertebrates over a 25-year period: Global Change Biology, v. 13, p. 942-957.

Fancy, S.G., Gross, J.E., and Carter, S.L., 2009, Monitoring the condition of natural resources in U.S. National Parks: Environmental Monitoring and Assessment, v. 151, p. 161–174.

Feminella, J.W., 1996, Comparison of benthic macroinvertebrate assemblages in small streams along a gradient in flow permanence: Journal of the North American Benthological Society, v. 15, p. 651–669.

Frissell, C.A., Liss, W.J., Warren, C.E., and Hurley, M.D. 1986, A hierarchical framework for stream habitat classification: Viewing streams in a watershed context: Environmental Management, v. 10, p. 199–214.

Grant, E.H.C., Lowe, W.H., and Fagan, W.F., 2007, Living in the branches: Population dynmacis and ecological processes in dentritic networks: Ecological Letters, v. 10, p. 165–175.

Griffith, M.B., Barrows, E.M., and Perry, S.A., 1998, Lateral dispersal of adult aquatic insects (Plecoptera, Trichoptera) following emergence from headwater streams in forested Appalachian catchments: Annals of the Entomological Society of America, v. 91, p. 195–201.

Heino, Jani, Soininen, Janne, Lappalainen, Jyrki, and Virtanen, Risto, 2005, The relationship between species richness and taxonomic distinctness in freshwater organism: Limnology and Oceanography, v. 50, p. 978–986.

Hongve, D., 1987, A revised procedure for discharge measurement by means of the salt dilution method: Hydrologic Processes, v. 1, p. 267–270.

Hughes, J.M., 2007, Constraints on recovery: Using molecular methods to study connectivity of aquatic biota in rivers and streams: Freshwater Biology, v. 52, p. 616–631.

Hughes, R.M., and Omernick, J.M., 1983, An alternative for characterizing stream size, in Fontaine, T.D., and Bartell, S.M., eds., Dynamics of lotic ecosystems: Ann Arbor, Mich., Ann Arbor Science, p. 87–102.

Hynes, H.B.N., 1975, The stream and its valley: Proceedings of the International Association of Theoretical and Applied Limnology, v. 19, p. 1–15.

Klemm, D.J., Blocksom, D.A., Fulk, F.A., Herlihy, A.T., Hughes, R.M., Kaufmann, P.R., Peck, D.V., Stoddard, J.L., Theony, W.T., and Griffity, M.B., 2003, Development and evaluation of a macroinvertebrate biotic integrity index (MBII) for regionally assessing mid-Atlantic highland streams: Environmental Management, v. 31, p. 656–669.

Klemm, D.J., Blocksom, K.A., Thoeny, W.T., Fullk, F.A., Herlihy, A.T., Kaufmann, P.R., and Cormier, S.M., 2002, Methods development and use of macroinvetebrates as indicators of ecological condition for streams in the Mid-Atlantic Highlands Region: Environmental Monitoring and Assessment, v. 78, p. 169–212.

Leopold, L.B., 1994, A View of the River: Cambridge, Mass., Harvard University Press, 298 pp.

Lowe, W.H., and Likens, G.E., 2005, Moving headwater streams to the head of the class: BioScience, v. 55, p. 196–197.

Maidment, D.R., ed., 2002, ArcHydro: GIS for Water Resources: Redlands, Calif., ESRI Press, 203 p.

Malmqvist, B., and Hoffsten, P., 2000, Macroinvertebrate taxonomic richness, community structure, and nestedness in Swedish streams: Archiv fur Hydrobiologie, v. 150, p. 29–54.

McCune, B., and Grace, J.B., 2002, Analysis of ecological communities: Gleneden Beach, Oreg., MJM Sofware Design, 300 pp.

Megan, M.H., Nash, M.S., Neale, A.C., and Pitchford. A.M., 2007, Biological integrity in Mid-Atlantic Coastal Plains headwater streams: Environmental Monitoring and Assessment, v. 124, p. 141–156.

Merrit, R.W., and Cummins, K.W., eds., 1996. Aquatic insects of North America: Dubuque, Iowa, Kendall/Hunt Publishing, 722 pp.

Meyer, J.L., Strayer, D.L., Wallace, J.B., Eggert, S.L., Helfman, G.S., and Leonard, N.E., 2007, The contribution of headwater streams to biodiversity in river networks: Journal of the American Water Resources Association, v. 43, p. 86–103.

Moeykens, M.D., and Voshell, Jr., J.R., 2002, Studies of benthic macroinvertebrates for the Shenandoah National Park long-term ecological monitoring system: Statistical analysis of LTEMS aquatic dataset from 1986 to 2000 on water chemistry, habitat, and macroinvertebrates: Virginia Tech Project Report No. 208-11-110A-007-374-1 (FRS#432535). 49 pp.

Monaghan, M.T., Robinson, C.T., Spaak, P., and Ward, J.V., 2005, Macroinvertebrate diversity in fragmented Alpine streams: Implications for freshwater conservation: Aquatic Science, v. 67, p. 454–464.

Morgan, B.A., Eaton, L.S., and Wieczorek, G.F., 2004, Pleistocene and Holocene colluvial fans and terraces in the Blue Ridge Region of Shenandoah National Park, Virginia: U.S. Geological Survey Open-File Report 2003–410, 25 p., 1 sheet, scale 1:100,000.

Mulholland, P.J., 1993, Hydrometric and stream chemistry evidence of three storm flowpaths in Walker Branch Watershed: Journal of Hydrology, v. 151, p. 291–316.

National Park Service, 1998, Resource Management Plan, 1998, Shenandoah National Park: Luray, Va., National Park Service.

Peterson, B.J., Wollheim, W.M., Mulholland, P.J., Webster, J.R., Meyer, J.L., Tank, J.L., Marti, E., Bowden, W.B., Valett, H.M., Hershey, A.E., McDowell, W.H., Dodds, W.K., Hamilton, S.K., Gregory, S., and Morrall, D.D., 2001, Control of nitrogen export from watersheds by headwater streams: Science, v. 292, p. 86–90.

Plummer, L.N., Busenberg, E., Bohlke, J.K., Carmody, R.W., Casile, G.C., Coplen, T.B., Doughten, M.W., Hannon, J.E., Kirkland, W., Michel, R.L., Nelms, D.L., Norton, B.C., Plummer, K.E., Qi, H., Revesz, K., Schlosser, P., Spitzer, S., Wayland, J.E., and Widman, P.K., 2000, Chemical and isotopic composition of water from springs, wells, and streams in parts of Shenandoah National Park, Virginia, and vicinity, 1995–1999: U.S. Geological Survey Open-File Report 2000–373, 70 p.

Rivenbark, B.L., and Jackson, C.R., 2004, Average discharge, perennial flow initiation, and channel initiation—small southern Applachian basins: Journal of the American Water Resources Association, v. 40, p. 639–646.

Snyder, C.D., Hitt, N.P., Smith, D.R., and Daily, J., in press, Evaluating bioassessment designs and decision thresholds using simulation techniques, *in* Gutenspergen, G., ed., Application of threshold concepts in natural resource decision making: New York, Springer Publishing.

Sullivan, T.J., Cosby, B.J., Laurence, J.A., Dennis, R.L., Savig, K., Webb, J.R., Bulger, A.J., Scruggs, M., Gordon, C., Ray, J., Lee, E.H., Hogsett, W.E., Wayne, H., Miller, D., and Kern, J.S., 2003, Assessment of air quality and related values in Shenandoah National Park: Philadelphia, Pa., U.S. Department of the Interior, NPS/NERCHAL/NRTR-03/090, 31pp.

Sullivan, T.J., Cosby, B.J., Webb, J.R., Dennis, R.L., Bulger, A.J., and Deviney Jr., F.A., 2008, Streamwater acid-base chemistry and critical loads of atmospheric deposition in Shenandoah National Park, Virginia: Environmental Monitoring and Assessment, 137, p. 85–99.

Townsend, C.R., 1989, The patch dynamics concept of stream communities: Journal of the North American Benthological Society, v. 8, p. 36–50.

Vana-Miller, D.L., and Weeks, D.P., 2004, Shenandoah National Park, Virginia, water resources scoping report, Technical Report, NPS/NRWRS/NRTR-2004/320, National Park Service, Water Resources Division, Fort Collins, CO. 138 pp.

Vannote, R.L., Minshall, G.W., Cummins, K.W., Sedell, J.R., and Cushing, C.E., 1980, The river continuum concept: Canadian Journal of Fisheries and Aquatic Sciences, v. 37, p. 130–137.

Vinson, M.R., and Hawkins, C.P., 1998, Biodiversity of stream insects: Variation at local, basin, and regional scales: Annual Review of Entolmology, v. 43, p. 271–293.

Wallace, J.B., Eggert, S.L., Meyer, J.L., and Webster, J.R., 1997, Multiple trophic levels of a forest stream linked to terrestrial litter inputs: Science, v. 277, p. 102–104.

Webb, R., Crosby, J., Deviney, F., Galloway, J., and Maben, S., 2011, Shenandoah National Park water quality and quantity monitoring protocol: Unpublished report, National Park Service, Shenandoah National Park, Natural Resources Management, 3655 Highway 211, East Luray, VA 22835. 45 pp.

Winter, T.C., Harvey, J.W., Franke, O.L., and Alley, W.M., 1998, Ground water and surface water, a single resource: U.S. Geological Survey, Circular 1139, Denver, CO. 79 pp.

Wofford, J.E.B., Voshell, J.R., and Demarest. E.D., 2011, Shenandoah National Park aquatic macroinvertebrate monitoring protocol: Unpublished report, National Park Service, Shenandoah National Park, Natural Resources Management, 3655 Highway 211, East Luray, VA 22835. 118 pp.

Wofford, J.E.B., and Demarest, E.D., 2011, Shenandoah National Park fish monitoring protocol, version 2.2: Unpublished report, National Park Service, Shenandoah National Park, Natural Resources Management, 3655 Highway 211, East Luray, VA 22835. 108 pp.

Wolock, D.M., Fan, J., and Lawrence, G.B., 1997, Effects of basin size on low-flow stream chemistry and subsurface contact time in the Neversink River Watershed, New York: Hydrologic Processes, v. 11, p. 1273–1286.

Young, J., Fleming, G., Townsend, P., and Lea, C., 2009, Vegetation of Shenandoah National Park in relation to environmental gradients, Version 2.0: Technical Report NPS/NER/NRTR-2009/142, National Park Service, Philadelphia, PA. 86 pp. plus appendices.

Appendix A. Description of macroinvertebrate taxa collected at 54 sites in Shenandoah National Park in 2007 and 2008.

[Appendix contains taxonomic descriptions as well as taxon-specific ecological characteristics required to compute benthic-macroinvertebrate summary statistics described in table 4 of this report.]

TAXON[1]	Phylum	Class	Order	Family	Genus	FUNC GRP[2]	TV[3]	HABIT[4]
5060	PLATYHELMINTHES	TURBELLARIA	TRICLADIDA	PLANARIIDAE		CG	8	SP
6000	NEMATODA					CG	8	BU
D2	ANNELIDA	OLIGOCHAETA				CG	8	BU
E08101	ARTHROPODA	CRUSTACEA	ISOPODA	ASELLIDAE	Caecidotea	CG	8	SP
E09300	ARTHROPODA	CRUSTACEA	AMPHIPODA		Crangonyx	CG	6	CR
E0A004	ARTHROPODA	CRUSTACEA	DECAPODA	CAMBARIDAE	Cambarus	GN	5	GN
E10001	ARTHROPODA	INSECTA	PLECOPTERA	PTERONARCYIDAE	Pteronarcys	SH	1	CR
E10100	ARTHROPODA	INSECTA	PLECOPTERA	PELTOPERLIDAE	Peltoperla	SH	1	CR
E10101	ARTHROPODA	INSECTA	PLECOPTERA	PELTOPERLIDAE	Tallaperla	SH	1	CR
E10210	ARTHROPODA	INSECTA	PLECOPTERA	NEMOURIDAE	Amphinemura	SH	3	CR
E10301	ARTHROPODA	INSECTA	PLECOPTERA	PERLIDAE	Paragnetina	PR	2	CR
E10302	ARTHROPODA	INSECTA	PLECOPTERA	PERLIDAE	Agnetina	PR	0	CR
E10313	ARTHROPODA	INSECTA	PLECOPTERA	PERLIDAE	Acroneuria	PR	2	CR
E10314	ARTHROPODA	INSECTA	PLECOPTERA	PERLIDAE	Eccoptura	PR	3	CR
E10315	ARTHROPODA	INSECTA	PLECOPTERA	PERLIDAE	Perlesta	PR	5	CR
E10401	ARTHROPODA	INSECTA	PLECOPTERA	PERLODIDAE	Yugus	PR	0	CR
E10404	ARTHROPODA	INSECTA	PLECOPTERA	PERLODIDAE	Remenus	PR	0	CR
E10411	ARTHROPODA	INSECTA	PLECOPTERA	PERLODIDAE	Isoperla	PR	2	CR
E10511	ARTHROPODA	INSECTA	PLECOPTERA	CHLOROPERLIDAE	Haploperla	PR	1	CR
E10512	ARTHROPODA	INSECTA	PLECOPTERA	CHLOROPERLIDAE	Sweltsa	PR	0	CR
E10700	ARTHROPODA	INSECTA	PLECOPTERA	LEUCTRIDAE	Leuctra	SH	0	CR
E10801	ARTHROPODA	INSECTA	PLECOPTERA	CAPNIIDAE	Paracapnia	SH	1	CR
E11000	ARTHROPODA	INSECTA	EPHEMEROPTERA	EPHEMERIDAE	Ephemera	CG	4	BU
E11303	ARTHROPODA	INSECTA	EPHEMEROPTERA	EPHEMERELLIDAE	Drunella	SC	0	CR

42

Appendix A (continued).

TAXA[1]	Phylum	Class	Order	Family	Genus	FUNC GRP[2]	TV[3]	HABIT[4]
E11304	ARTHROPODA	INSECTA	EPHEMEROPTERA	EPHEMERELLIDAE	*Ephemerella*	CG	2	CR
E11305	ARTHROPODA	INSECTA	EPHEMEROPTERA	EPHEMERELLIDAE	*Eurylophella*	CG	4	CR
E11500	ARTHROPODA	INSECTA	EPHEMEROPTERA	AMELETIDAE	*Ameletus*	SC	1	CG
E11601	ARTHROPODA	INSECTA	EPHEMEROPTERA	LEPTOPHLEBIIDAE	*Paraleptophlebia*	CG	1	CR
E11603	ARTHROPODA	INSECTA	EPHEMEROPTERA	LEPTOPHLEBIIDAE	*Habrophlebia*	CG	1	CR
E11604	ARTHROPODA	INSECTA	EPHEMEROPTERA	LEPTOPHLEBIIDAE	*Habrophlebiodes*	SC	1	CR
E11701	ARTHROPODA	INSECTA	EPHEMEROPTERA	BAETIDAE	*Baetis*	CG	5	CG
E11707	ARTHROPODA	INSECTA	EPHEMEROPTERA	BAETIDAE	*Acerpenna*	CG	5	CG
E1170Z	ARTHROPODA	INSECTA	EPHEMEROPTERA	BAETIDAE	*Baetis (complex)*	CG	5	CG
E11900	ARTHROPODA	INSECTA	EPHEMEROPTERA	HEPTAGENIIDAE	*Stenonema*	SC	4	CG
E11901	ARTHROPODA	INSECTA	EPHEMEROPTERA	HEPTAGENIIDAE	*Stenacron*	CG	4	CG
E11902	ARTHROPODA	INSECTA	EPHEMEROPTERA	HEPTAGENIIDAE	*Epeorus*	CG	1	CG
E11903	ARTHROPODA	INSECTA	EPHEMEROPTERA	HEPTAGENIIDAE	*Cinygmula*	SC	1	CG
E11904	ARTHROPODA	INSECTA	EPHEMEROPTERA	HEPTAGENIIDAE	*Leucrocuta*	SC	2	CG
E11905	ARTHROPODA	INSECTA	EPHEMEROPTERA	HEPTAGENIIDAE	*Heptagenia*	SC	3	CG
E11D04	ARTHROPODA	INSECTA	EPHEMEROPTERA	ISONYCHIIDAE	*Isonychia*	CF	3	CG
E12000	ARTHROPODA	INSECTA	ODONATA	ANISOPTERA	*Cordulegaster*	PR	3	BU
E12029	ARTHROPODA	INSECTA	ODONATA	ANISOPTERA	*Lanthus*	PR	1	BU
E12053	ARTHROPODA	INSECTA	ODONATA	ANISOPTERA	*Somatochlora*	PR	8	CL
E13400	ARTHROPODA	INSECTA	HEMIPTERA	VELIIDAE	*Microvelia*	PR	8	SK
E14000	ARTHROPODA	INSECTA	MEGALOPTERA	SIALIDAE	*Sialis*	PR	7	SP
E14111	ARTHROPODA	INSECTA	MEGALOPTERA	CORYDALIDAE	*Nigronia*	PR	4	CR
E16012	ARTHROPODA	INSECTA	TRICHOPTERA	HYDROPTILIDAE	*Hydroptila*	MP	6	CR
E16210	ARTHROPODA	INSECTA	TRICHOPTERA	HYDROPSYCHIDAE	*Hydropsyche*	CF	6	CG
E16211	ARTHROPODA	INSECTA	TRICHOPTERA	HYDROPSYCHIDAE	*Cheumatopsyche*	CF	6	CG
E16220	ARTHROPODA	INSECTA	TRICHOPTERA	HYDROPSYCHIDAE	*Diplectrona*	CF	2	CG
E16230	ARTHROPODA	INSECTA	TRICHOPTERA	HYDROPSYCHIDAE	*Parapsyche*	CF	2	CG

43

Appendix A (continued).

TAXA[1]	Phylum	Class	Order	Family	Genus	FUNC GRP[2]	TV[3]	HABIT[4]
E16300	ARTHROPODA	INSECTA	TRICHOPTERA	RHYACOPHILIDAE	*Rhyacophila*	PR	1	CR
E16400	ARTHROPODA	INSECTA	TRICHOPTERA	PHILOPOTAMIDAE	*Chimarra*	CF	3	CG
E16410	ARTHROPODA	INSECTA	TRICHOPTERA	PHILOPOTAMIDAE	*Wormaldia*	CF	1	CG
E16411	ARTHROPODA	INSECTA	TRICHOPTERA	PHILOPOTAMIDAE	*Dolophilodes*	CF	1	CG
E16501	ARTHROPODA	INSECTA	TRICHOPTERA	PSYCHOMYIIDAE	*Lype*	SC	4	CG
E167	ARTHROPODA	INSECTA	TRICHOPTERA	LEPTOCERIDAE		CG	4	CR
E16A00	ARTHROPODA	INSECTA	TRICHOPTERA	ODONTOCERIDAE	*Psilotreta*	SC	0	CG
E16C00	ARTHROPODA	INSECTA	TRICHOPTERA	BRACHYCENTRIDAE	*Micrasema*	SH	1	CG
E16C01	ARTHROPODA	INSECTA	TRICHOPTERA	BRACHYCENTRIDAE	*Brachycentrus*	CF	1	CR
E16E00	ARTHROPODA	INSECTA	TRICHOPTERA	LEPIDOSTOMATIDAE	*Lepidostoma*	SH	1	CG
E16F00	ARTHROPODA	INSECTA	TRICHOPTERA	GLOSSOSOMATIDAE	*Glossosoma*	SC	0	CG
E16F10	ARTHROPODA	INSECTA	TRICHOPTERA	GLOSSOSOMATIDAE	*Agapetus*	SC	0	CR
E16G10	ARTHROPODA	INSECTA	TRICHOPTERA	LIMNEPHILIDAE	*Pycnopsyche*	SH	4	CG
E16H01	ARTHROPODA	INSECTA	TRICHOPTERA	POLYCENTROPODIDAE	*Neureclipsis*	CF	4	SP
E16H02	ARTHROPODA	INSECTA	TRICHOPTERA	POLYCENTROPODIDAE	*Nyctiophylax*	PR	3	CG
E16H03	ARTHROPODA	INSECTA	TRICHOPTERA	POLYCENTROPODIDAE	*Polycentropus*	PR	4	SP
E16H04	ARTHROPODA	INSECTA	TRICHOPTERA	POLYCENTROPODIDAE	*Cernotina*	PR	4	SP
E16100	ARTHROPODA	INSECTA	TRICHOPTERA	MOLANNIDAE	*Molanna*	SC	6	SP
E16J00	ARTHROPODA	INSECTA	TRICHOPTERA	SERICOSTOMATIDAE	*Fattigia*	SH	1	CG
E16M00	ARTHROPODA	INSECTA	TRICHOPTERA	UENOIDAE	*Neophylax*	SC	2	
E17	ARTHROPODA	INSECTA	LEPIDOPTERA				8	GN
E18220	ARTHROPODA	INSECTA	COLEOPTERA	DYTISCIDAE	*Hydroporus*	PR	6	GN
E18400	ARTHROPODA	INSECTA	COLEOPTERA	HYDROPHILIDAE	*Tropisternus*	PR	7	GN
E18460	ARTHROPODA	INSECTA	COLEOPTERA	HYDROPHILIDAE	*Hydrobius*	SH	8	CG
E18700	ARTHROPODA	INSECTA	COLEOPTERA	PSEPHENIDAE	*Psephenus*	SC	4	CG
E18701	ARTHROPODA	INSECTA	COLEOPTERA	PSEPHENIDAE	*Ectopria*	SC	4	CG
E18900	ARTHROPODA	INSECTA	COLEOPTERA	ELMIDAE	*Stenelmis*	SC	5	

Appendix A (continued).

TAXA[1]	Phylum	Class	Order	Family	Genus	FUNC GRP[2]	TV[3]	HABIT[4]
E18904	ARTHROPODA	INSECTA	COLEOPTERA	ELMIDAE	*Optioservus*	SC	5	CG
E18906	ARTHROPODA	INSECTA	COLEOPTERA	ELMIDAE	*Promoresia*	SC	2	CG
E18907	ARTHROPODA	INSECTA	COLEOPTERA	ELMIDAE	*Oulimnius*	SC	2	CG
E18D	ARTHROPODA	INSECTA	COLEOPTERA	STAPHYLINIDAE		PR	5	CG
E19000	ARTHROPODA	INSECTA	DIPTERA	BLEPHARICERIDAE	*Blepharicera*	SC	0	CG
E19200	ARTHROPODA	INSECTA	DIPTERA	TIPULIDAE	*Tipula*	SH	5	BU
E19205	ARTHROPODA	INSECTA	DIPTERA	TIPULIDAE	*Brachypremna*	SH	4	BU
E19210	ARTHROPODA	INSECTA	DIPTERA	TIPULIDAE	*Antocha*	CG	3	CG
E19211	ARTHROPODA	INSECTA	DIPTERA	TIPULIDAE	*Limonia*	SH	6	BU
E19220	ARTHROPODA	INSECTA	DIPTERA	TIPULIDAE	*Dicranota*	PR	3	CR
E19221	ARTHROPODA	INSECTA	DIPTERA	TIPULIDAE	*Pedicia*	PR	4	BU
E19230	ARTHROPODA	INSECTA	DIPTERA	TIPULIDAE	*Hexatoma*	PR	3	CR
E19231	ARTHROPODA	INSECTA	DIPTERA	TIPULIDAE	*Limnophila*	PR	4	BU
E19232	ARTHROPODA	INSECTA	DIPTERA	TIPULIDAE	*Pseudolimnophila*	PR	7	BU
E19234	ARTHROPODA	INSECTA	DIPTERA	TIPULIDAE	*Pilaria*	PR	3	BU
E19235	ARTHROPODA	INSECTA	DIPTERA	TIPULIDAE	*Dactylolabis*	PR	3	BU
E19241	ARTHROPODA	INSECTA	DIPTERA	TIPULIDAE	*Molophilus*	CG	3	BU
E19242	ARTHROPODA	INSECTA	DIPTERA	TIPULIDAE	*Ormosia*	CG	4	BU
E19243	ARTHROPODA	INSECTA	DIPTERA	TIPULIDAE	*Erioptera*	CG	3	BU
E19311	ARTHROPODA	INSECTA	DIPTERA	PSYCHODIDAE	*Pericoma*	CG	10	BU
E19500	ARTHROPODA	INSECTA	DIPTERA	DIXIDAE	*Dixa*	CG	3	CR
E19700	ARTHROPODA	INSECTA	DIPTERA	SIMULIIDAE	*Prosimulium*	CF	4	CG
E19720	ARTHROPODA	INSECTA	DIPTERA	SIMULIIDAE	*Simulium*	CF	6	CG
E198	ARTHROPODA	INSECTA	DIPTERA	CHIRONOMIDAE		CG	6	BU
E19901	ARTHROPODA	INSECTA	DIPTERA	CERATOPOGONIDAE	*Forcipomyia*	SC	6	SP
E19922	ARTHROPODA	INSECTA	DIPTERA	CERATOPOGONIDAE	*Bezzia*	PR	6	BU
E19925	ARTHROPODA	INSECTA	DIPTERA	CERATOPOGONIDAE	*Ceratopogon*	PR	6	BU

Appendix A (continued).

TAXA[1]	Phylum	Class	Order	Family	Genus	FUNC GRP[2]	TV[3]	HABIT[4]
E19926	ARTHROPODA	INSECTA	DIPTERA	CERATOPOGONIDAE	*Probezzia*	PR	6	BU
E19A10	ARTHROPODA	INSECTA	DIPTERA	STRATIOMYIIDAE	*Odontomyia*	CG	10	SP
E19B00	ARTHROPODA	INSECTA	DIPTERA	TABANIDAE	*Chrysops*	CG	7	BU
E19J00	ARTHROPODA	INSECTA	DIPTERA	EMPIDIDAE	*Hemerodromia*	PR	6	CR
E19J01	ARTHROPODA	INSECTA	DIPTERA	EMPIDIDAE	*Chelifera*	PR	6	SP
E19J10	ARTHROPODA	INSECTA	DIPTERA	EMPIDIDAE	*Clinocera*	PR	6	CG
E19J30	ARTHROPODA	INSECTA	DIPTERA	EMPIDIDAE	*Oreogeton*	PR	6	SP
E19K	ARTHROPODA	INSECTA	DIPTERA	MUSCIDAE		PR	8	SP
E1A0	ARTHROPODA	INSECTA	COLLEMBOLA	PODURIDAE		CG	7	SK
E1A2	ARTHROPODA	INSECTA	COLLEMBOLA	ISOTOMIDAE		CG	7	SK
E1A3	ARTHROPODA	INSECTA	COLLEMBOLA	ENTOMOBRYIDAE		CG	7	SK
E1A4	ARTHROPODA	INSECTA	COLLEMBOLA	ONYCHIURIDAE		CG	7	SK
E20	ARTHROPODA	ARACHNIDA	ACARI			PR	6	CR
F0	MOLLUSCA	GASTROPODA				SC	8	
F110	MOLLUSCA	BIVALVIA	VENEROIDA	SPHAERIIDAE		CF	8	BU

[1]Taxa Codes were derived from those contained in Shenandoah National Park long-term monitoring database provided to U.S. Geological Survey in Microsoft Access file "USGS_All_Stream_Data_2010"; table "W_Alzdd_Taxa."

[2]Functional groups were derived from those contained in Shenandoah National Park long-term monitoring database provided to U.S. Geological Survey in Microsoft Access file "USGS_All_Stream_Data_2010"; table "W_Alzdd_Taxa." Functional groups are as follows: CF=Collector filterer; CG=Collector-gatherer; GN=Generalist feeder; MP=Macrophyte piercer; PR=Predator; SC=Scraper; and SH=shredder. These characteristics were used to compute community metrics %Shredders and %Scrapers (see table 4).

[3]Tolerance values were derived from those contained in Shenandoah National Park long-term monitoring database provided to U.S. Geological Survey in Microsoft Access file "USGS_All_Stream_Data_2010"; table "W_Alzdd_Taxa.". These values were used to compute community pollution tolerance values (see table 4).

[4]Taxon-specific "habits" were derived from those contained in Shenandoah National Park long-term monitoring database provided to U.S. Geological Survey in Microsoft Access file "USGS_All_Stream_Data_2010"; table "W_Alzdd_Taxa." Habit codes are as follows: BU=Burrowers; CG=Climbers; CL=Climbers; DV=Divers; GN=Generalist; SK=Skaters; and SP=Sprawlers. These characteristics were used to compute the community metric "%Hapto (Haptobenthos), which is the sum of crawlers and clingers (see table 4).

www.ingramcontent.com/pod-product-compliance
Lightning Source LLC
Chambersburg PA
CBHW080450290526
45791CB00008BA/2668